PEA RIDGE AND PRAIRIE GROVE

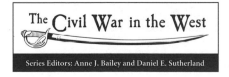

The Civil War in the West

Series Editors: Anne J. Bailey and Daniel E. Sutherland

PEA RIDGE AND PRAIRIE GROVE;

OR,

SCENES AND INCIDENTS

OF THE

WAR IN ARKANSAS

BY

WILLIAM BAXTER

INTRODUCTION BY WILLIAM L. SHEA

University of Arkansas Press
Fayetteville
2000

Library of Congress Cataloging-in-Publication Data

Baxter, William, 1820–1880.
    Pea Ridge and Prairie Grove, or, Scenes and incidents of the war in Arkansas / William Baxter ; introduction by William L. Shea.
        p. cm.– (The Civil War in the West)
    Originally published: Cincinnati : Poe & Hitchcock, 1864.
    ISBN 1-55728-591-8 (pbk.)
    1. Arkansas–History–Civil War, 1861–1865. 2. Fayetteville Region (Ark.)–History, Military–19th century. I.Title: Pea Ridge and Prairie Grove. II. Title: Scenes and incidents of the war in Arkansas. III. Title. IV. Series.

E496+
973.7'09767–dc21
                                                                  99-059554

Reprinted from the original edition published in 1864 by Poe & Hitchcock. A introduction has been added to this edition. Some regularization in spelling and punctuation in the text has been made by the University of Arkansas Press.

Cover photograph of Fayetteville courtesy Shiloh Museum of Ozark History. Frontispiece photograph of William Baxter courtesy Washington County Historial Society/Shiloh Museum of Ozark History.

CONTENTS

Series Editors' Preface
ix

Introduction by William L. Shea
xi

CHAPTER I.
INTRODUCTORY.
Reasons for writing—My two friends—Knowledge of the
Southern country and people—Election of Lincoln and its
immediate results—The Doctor and Senator
1

CHAPTER II.
PATTING THE TIGER.
Course pursued by Union men—Why we did not leave at the
first outbreak—Scenes in college—Students enlisting—
Fate of my pupils
10

CHAPTER III.
ROMANCE AND REALITY.
Southern boasting—Hempstead Rifles—Waking up—
Wilson's Creek—Price's retreat—Sacking the town
16

CHAPTER IV.
BURNING THE TOWN.
Among the bombshells—A critical moment—A cavalry
charge—Under the old flag again—A sad incident
24

CHAPTER V.
IN PRISON.

Judge Tebbetts arrested—My own narrow escape—A Union
woman's trials—Tebbetts before M'Culloch—A false friend—
A true friend—The presentiment—The trial and release
32

CHAPTER VI.
BATTLE OF PEA RIDGE.

The Confederates advance—They meet Sigel—Death of
M'Culloch and M'Intosh—News from the field—Flight of the
army southward—The sharp-shooter
42

CHAPTER VII.
SECESSION PREACHERS.

Todd—Mitchell—Caples—Speech by a layman—
A warlike chaplain
50

CHAPTER VIII.
GUERRILLAS.

Roving bands—The midnight murder—Smith and his
negroes—Assassination of Neal—Retaliation
61

CHAPTER IX.
REBELS—RUMORS—RAIDS.

Secession orators—Marvelous stories—Escape of Tebbetts
and Graham—Weary days—Sick soldiers
71

CHAPTER X.
THE MARCH AND BATTLE.
The madman—The army and its doings—Gen. Herron's
forced march—Night before the battle—
Battle of Prairie Grove
81

CHAPTER XI.
AFTER THE BATTLE.
Arrival of the wounded—The hospitals—Fortitude of the
wounded—Deserters—Change of opinion—
Venus and Mars, or woman's wit
90

CHAPTER XII.
PEN PORTRAITS.
Changed scenes—The fickle—The bold—A Confederate
officer—Veterans—The major—A new convert—The true
man—The recreant—A hero—Last-ditch men
99

CHAPTER XIII.
PREPARING TO LEAVE.
Desolation—Removal necessary—Battle near my house—
Reasons for delay—Southern bitterness not general—
The future of the South
107

CHAPTER XIV.
ON THE ROAD.
Parting—Relief of mind—Night on Pea Ridge—Dead bush
whackers—Preaching—Our appearance at the close of our
trip—Disappointment—Daylight
116

SERIES EDITORS' PREFACE

The Civil War in the West has a single goal: To promote historical writing about the war in the western states and territories. It focuses most particularly on the Trans-Mississippi theater, which consisted of Missouri, Arkansas, Texas, most of Louisiana (west of the Mississippi River), Indian Territory (modern day Oklahoma), and Arizona Territory (two-fifths of modern day Arizona and New Mexico), but it also encompasses adjacent states, such as Kansas, Tennessee, and Mississippi, that directly influenced the Trans-Mississippi war. It is a wide swath, to be sure, but one too often ignored by historians and, consequently, too little understood and appreciated.

Topically, the series embraces all aspects of the wartime story. Military history in its many guises, from the strategies of generals to the daily lives of common soldiers, forms an important part of that story, but so, too, do the numerous and complex political, economic, social, and diplomatic dimensions of the war. The series also provides a variety of perspectives on these topics. Most importantly, it offers the best in modern scholarship, with thoughtful, challenging monographs. Secondly, it presents new editions of important books that have gone out of print. And thirdly, it premieres expertly edited correspondence, diaries, reminiscences, and other writings by witnesses to the war.

It is a formidable undertaking, but we believe that The Civil War in the West, by focusing on some of the least familiar dimensions of the conflict, significantly broadens understanding of that dramatic story.

William Baxter's classic *Pea Ridge and Prairie Grove*, published originally in 1864, is a firsthand account of two of the most famous Civil War campaigns in Arkansas. Baxter, an

Englishman by birth and a staunch Unionist, served as pastor of the Disciples of Christ in Fayetteville and as president of Arkansas College at the time of the dramatic events he describes. He did not witness the two battles, but he was a keen observer of the chaos created by the clash of armies in northwest Arkansas. The value of his testimony lies not so much in the details of military events—although he summarizes his conversations with military men—as in his wonderfully insightful portrayal of a community—Fayetteville and vicinity—caught in the vortex of war. It is the world of the noncombatant, besieged not only by rival armies but by roving bands of guerrillas, that Baxter so brilliantly explores. He vividly describes the physical scene, but he also conveys the emotions, thoughts, and attitudes of the people. He reports on hospitals filled with soldiers, military prisons, and the burning of the town, but he also recreates the tensions between soldiers and civilians and the clashes between neighbors whose loyalties divided them into warring camps, secessionist versus Unionist.

Such a text could well stand on its own, but it has been supplemented in this new edition by an authoritative and insightful introduction that places the book and its author in historical perspective. William L. Shea, professor of history at the University of Arkansas at Monticello, is the author of *War in the West: Pea Ridge and Prairie Grove* (1996) and co-author *of Pea Ridge: Civil War Campaign in the West* (1992). Currently at work on a detailed study of the Prairie Grove campaign, he is an acknowledged expert on the war in Arkansas. His thoughts on Baxter and the Civil War in northwest Arkansas make this edition of *Pea Ridge and Prairie Grove* a valuable research tool and a rewarding work of literature that will be applauded by both scholars and the general public.

Anne J. Bailey
Daniel E. Sutherland

INTRODUCTION

BY WILLIAM L. SHEA

"May you live in interesting times." So goes an old Chinese curse. William Baxter was one of millions of Americans condemned to live in very interesting times, indeed. Baxter was a resident of northwest Arkansas during the first half of the Civil War. He wrote about his experiences in *Pea Ridge and Prairie Grove; or, Scenes and Incidents of the War in Arkansas*, which was published in 1864 while the fighting still raged. The book is a remarkable account of the little-known conflict beyond the camping grounds and battlefields. It describes the horrific struggle for survival faced by people caught up in the secession crisis and the scourge that followed. For four years and more, hundreds of thousands of men, women, and children, nearly all of them residents of the upper South, suffered appalling hardships in an enormous no man's land that stretched a thousand miles from Kansas and the Indian Territory to Virginia and the Sea Islands. Unlike so many others who died or never had an opportunity to tell of their travails, Baxter survived and put his story down on paper.

William Baxter was born in Leeds, England, in 1820 and emigrated to the United States with his family eight years later. A deeply religious young man, Baxter joined the Methodist Church at the age of sixteen but only two years later turned to the Christian Church, or Disciples of Christ. After graduating from Bethany College in Virginia (now West Virginia) in 1845, he was ordained a minister in the Christian Church and entered upon a lifelong commitment to teaching and spreading the gospel.

Following a brief sojourn in Pennsylvania, Baxter, like millions of other Americans in the antebellum years, moved west and south down the broad valleys of the Ohio and the Mississippi. For a dozen years he ministered to congregations and taught schools in Port Gibson and Woodville, Mississippi, the latter town the boyhood home of a rising politician named Jefferson Davis.

Baxter's next place of work was quite a change from the hot, humid environs of the lower Mississippi Valley. In 1858, following a brief stint in Baton Rouge, duty called him to Fayetteville, Arkansas, a thriving frontier community perched atop the Ozark Plateau in northwest corner of the state. Despite its location only twenty-five miles from Indian Territory, Fayetteville was well on its way to becoming a seat of culture and learning. Baxter became pastor of a substantial congregation and president of Arkansas College, a school for men. He and his family lived next to the college in a one-story frame house with fashionable Greek revival detailing. The Baxter house is long gone, but the house directly across Dickson Street, believed to resemble its neighbor very closely, still survives. It is known locally as Headquarters House, and it was the home of Jonas M. Tebbets, who figures prominently in Baxter's narrative. The college, too, is gone, a victim of senseless Confederate vandalism, but the name of the busy thoroughfare it once faced, College Street, remains.

After fifteen years below the Mason-Dixon line, Baxter regarded the South as his home. But he had spent an equal number of years in the North, and he was familiar with northern attitudes toward the South. He knew that Arkansas, in particular, had an undeserved reputation as a wilderness populated by primitive hunters and trappers living on the edge of savagery. Baxter remarks in his book that "the impression has been very general that society in Arkansas was but one remove from barbarism," and he endeavored to rebut that unfortunate stereotype. (Stereotypes are notoriously resilient, however, and the distorted image of Arkansas that bothered Baxter still seems to be alive and well at the beginning of the twenty-first century.) Baxter points out, quite accurately, that prewar Fayetteville was a prosperous town graced with handsome homes, churches, public buildings, and institutions of higher learning, one of them his own.

Pea Ridge and Prairie Grove combines elements of a personal memoir and a record of events. The core of the book is Baxter's account of the turmoil caused by secession and war, and the tyranny imposed by the secessionist majority over the loyalist minority in what had been a peaceful community. Freedom of expression was soon extinguished in much of the Confederacy, including northwest Arkansas. Baxter was a prominent citizen used to stating his opinion from pulpit and lectern, but as the secession crisis boiled over in 1860 and 1861, it became increasingly dangerous to express Unionist sentiments in public. Unionism was relatively strong in the upper South, but secessionism was stronger still and tinged with a violent extremism. Baxter discovered who in Fayetteville was of like mind and who was not. Guarded looks and furtive conversations became the order of the day.

If that were not bad enough, Baxter had the misfortune to live in a town that changed hands a half-dozen times in the first eighteen months of the war. Baxter, his friend and neighbor Tebbets, and other Unionists welcomed as deliverers the first Union troops to reach Fayetteville, only to discover that the occupation was temporary. Their displays of loyalty to the old flag led to harassment, threats, arrest, and, ultimately, exile or death. Of course, vengeful secessionists did not fare much better in the long run, for the Confederate army could not hold Fayetteville either. Each episode of military occupation and abandonment produced a new hemorrhage of refugees fearing retribution by whichever side temporarily held the upper hand. By the end of the war the once lovely little town, vandalized almost beyond recognition, had become a depopulated shell.

Assessing the reliability of first-person accounts penned by aggrieved parties is always difficult, but several of the episodes Baxter describes can be verified by other sources. For example, he recounts the brief occupation of Fayetteville by Brig. Gen. Alexander S. Asboth's cavalry brigade on February 22–26, 1862, the first time the town was held by Union forces. Union records corroborate Baxter's account. A few pages later Baxter mentions in passing that "Our friend Wilson's son, a lad of fourteen, had his leg shot off" at Pea Ridge. An examination of Confederate records reveals that William Wilson of Fayetteville, age fourteen, attached himself to Capt. John J. Good's Texas Battery when it rumbled through town a few days before the battle. The unfortunate boy was struck by an artillery round on March 8, 1862, near the close of the battle and his shattered leg was amputated. Baxter probably should be considered a dependable source of information about life in wartime Fayetteville, at least when relating events that he personally witnessed or that he heard at firsthand from a select group of close friends. Unfortunately for historians, Baxter often declines to identify persons by name and simply refers to a "former friend" or "gentleman of the town."

Unequaled as a source of local history, Baxter's book is also a solid literary achievement. The narrative is earnest in tone, straightforward in organization, and easy for modern readers to follow. Humor and sarcasm are present on occasion, but there are fewer religious allusions than might be expected from a man of the cloth. From time to time Baxter gets briefly sidetracked by an odd or memorable episode, such as his sad tale of a soldier mentally unhinged by combat, but on the whole he keeps to his theme. The narrative is notable for its consistently one-sided descriptions of stalwart, long-suffering Unionists and their loud-mouthed, hypocritical, hateful oppressors. Baxter may have been accurate, but he was also partisan.

An interesting feature of Baxter's book is his depiction of "the coarse, brutal, and profane Texan," Brig. Gen. Benjamin

McCulloch, the Confederate commander in northwest Arkansas. Killed at Pea Ridge on March 7, 1862, McCulloch quickly
achieved the status of a saint, the common fate of "martyred"
Confederate general officers from Albert Sydney Johnston to
Thomas "Stonewall" Jackson. McCulloch's comrades in arms
spoke of him in glowing terms and bemoaned his untimely
death as the fatal blow to Confederate military hopes in the
Trans-Mississippi. The McCulloch described by Baxter was a
different creature altogether, a vulgar and vindictive military
tyrant.

At this distance it is difficult to say whether Baxter's ver-
sion of McCulloch is more accurate than that of the general's
hagiographers, but it is certain that Baxter had good reason to
despise the Confederate commander. McCulloch arrested and
threatened to kill Baxter's friend and fellow Unionist, Jonas
Tebbets. McCulloch also was responsible for burning much of
Fayetteville when Confederate troops abandoned the town on
February 21, 1862, an act that was as unnecessary as it was
shocking. Finally, and perhaps most telling, it apparently was
McCulloch who ordered the destruction by fire of Arkansas
College on the night of March 4 during the Rebel advance to
Pea Ridge. The conflagration set Baxter's own house afire, and
he barely managed to extinguish the flames. McCulloch's incin-
eration of much of Fayetteville during the Confederate retreat
might be excused as an unfortunate error in judgement, but the
wanton destruction of Arkansas College took place after the
Confederates re-occupied Fayetteville and were in the process
of regaining northwest Arkansas, or so they believed. No other
building in town was harmed. In Baxter's mind, McCulloch
destroyed the college—one of the premier educational institutions in Arkansas—in order to intimidate or punish the
college president, whose Unionist feelings had become public
knowledge.

Baxter condemns the Confederates for the havoc they
wreaked on Fayetteville, but he is only slightly less critical of

the blue-clad soldiers of Brig. Gen. John M. Schofield's army who ravaged the town in October 1862. Baxter discovered to his dismay that many Union troops did not distinguish between loyal and disloyal southerners, but looted and pillaged indiscriminately. The sack of Fayetteville was reflective of changing attitudes in the North and the emergence of a harder, more destructive kind of warfare that ultimately devastated the South. The return of Union forces to northwest Arkansas led to a second battle, Prairie Grove, fought ten miles west of town on December 7. Baxter describes the flood of wounded soldiers that poured into Fayetteville and his own pathetically inadequate efforts to comfort them.

After Pea Ridge and Prairie Grove the armies gradually moved away to the east, never to return, but a new form of terror swept over northwest Arkansas in the form of outlaws, guerrillas, and ill-disciplined cavalrymen in blue and gray who often were indistinguishable from freebooters. Murders and other atrocities became commonplace as the struggle spiraled downward into savagery. Fayetteville grew increasingly isolated and the specter of famine appeared. In a few pithy phrases Baxter aptly sums up the impact of eighteen months of true civil war on northwest Arkansas: "Schools and institutions of learning broken up, churches abandoned, the Sabbath unnoted, every thing around, indeed, denoting a rapid lapse into barbarism, all trade at an end, nearly all travel suspended, the comforts of life nearly all gone, the absolute necessaries difficult to be obtained, altogether made a picture difficult to be realized in a country which has not been made the scene of war." It was all too much for Baxter. Penniless and in constant fear for his life, he accompanied a Union wagon train out of Fayetteville in February 1863.

Baxter's account ends with his flight to St. Louis and from there to Cincinnati. During the first year of his exile Baxter produced a history of his recent experiences, but the tale of personal travails in Arkansas received little notice when the public's attention was riveted on the titanic military campaigns then underway in Georgia and Virginia. Perhaps Baxter expected as much. He slowly recovered from the loss of his home and livelihood in Arkansas and resumed his ministry in Ohio. His health weakened by wartime trials and tribulations, Baxter died in 1880 at the age of sixty.

Baxter was a prolific writer, and he published a great many essays of a religious or contemplative nature, but his account of the calamity that swept across northwest Arkansas is his most significant work. By the middle of the twentieth century, however, only a handful of copies of *Pea Ridge and Prairie Grove* were known to exist. When the Civil War centennial approached, Hugh Park, publisher of the Van Buren, Arkansas, *Press-Argus*, reprinted Baxter's book in a limited edition in 1957. As the century wore on, Park's facsimile edition became almost as rare as the original. With the publication of this paperback edition by the University of Arkansas Press as part of its series on the Civil War in the West, *Pea Ridge and Prairie Grove* finally will receive the attention it deserves, and more light will be shed on a dark and dismal period in American history.

PEA RIDGE AND PRAIRIE GROVE;

OR,

SCENES AND INCIDENTS

OF THE

WAR IN ARKANSAS

BY

WILLIAM BAXTER

PEA RIDGE AND PRAIRIE GROVE.

CHAPTER I.

INTRODUCTORY.

Reasons for writing—My two friends—Knowledge of the
Southern country and people—Election of Lincoln and its
immediate results—The Doctor and Senator.

TO few persons have the past three years possessed such
varied interest as to the writer of these pages; and yet were that
an individual interest only, they would never have been written. But the fact, that other histories have been interwoven
with my own, and that many things which else would have been
forever unsaid will of necessity be written here, has impelled me
to this undertaking; and while I describe scenes which never
will pass from my memory, I indulge the hope that the impression will be made, that the rebellion has developed a heroism
on the part of many Union men in the South, not inferior to
that exhibited on the bloodiest fields of the war.

Having lived nearly two years in a region occupied alternately by the Confederate and Union forces, and from my social
position enjoying superior advantages for observation, I have

no hesitancy in saying, that I am one of the only three persons by whom the events to be narrated could be written; and no one of the three could give his own history during those years without ever and anon bringing in that of the other two; and to weave into the thread of my story the doings and sufferings of those noble men is with me a labor of love; for though one was the earliest and best-known friend of my life, and the other one whom the intercourse of my maturer manhood, when the heart opens cautiously to new friends, compelled me to receive without a doubt, yet I never knew them fully till their true nature was revealed by the unfailing test of a common suffering and a common danger.

But when was tale ever penned around which great interest gathers, from the sad scene in Eden to the more sorrowful one at the Cross, in which woman did not play a part? nor will this humble story form the exception; for there were wives and mothers well known to me, who amid trials not inferior, as facts will show, to those passed through by the fair Pilgrims in the Mayflower, or the women of the Revolution, bore them as nobly and as uncomplainingly as they.

As it is my purpose to give a narrative of facts, it will not be improper to say that the two persons to whom I have alluded are, first, Hon. J. M. Tebbetts, a lawyer and politician of distinction, a native of New Hampshire, but for more than twenty years a resident of Arkansas, a man of wealth, education, and influence, and of what spirit to carry out his convictions the following pages will show; the other, Elder Robert Graham, a man widely known, admired, and beloved, not only in the State of his adoption, but also in Missouri, Louisiana, and Texas, and, without exception, the most earnest, indefatigable, and successful laborer in the cause of education and religion in the South-West.

In the Fall of 1860 we were all living at Fayetteville, Washington county, Arkansas, a beautiful village of nearly two thousand inhabitants, the seat of two large and flourishing female seminaries, and also of Arkansas College, an institution projected by Elder Graham, and by his untiring efforts brought to a very high degree of usefulness and efficiency, having numbered at one time, under his administration, nearly two hundred students, many of them from Louisiana and Missouri; indeed, for hundreds of miles around, there was no institution at all comparable to it; many blessings had already flowed from it, and hopes, many and bright, clustered around its future. At this period the writer was President of Arkansas College and pastor of a congregation worshiping in the most beautiful and commodious church in that region. Attached to it was a Sunday school, which, with abundant opportunity for comparison, I believe was one of the best I ever saw. True, I have seen much larger schools both North and South, but for zeal and promptitude, for deep and lasting interest, I have not seen it surpassed. The early New England training of Judge Tebbetts qualified him admirably for the oversight of such a school; and though lawyer and politician, neither his profession nor his party ever caused him to forget that school. I have been thus particular from the fact that the impression has been very general that society in Arkansas was but one remove from barbarism: in some portions, doubtless, the people are rude and rough, but I have never yet in my travels, which have extended from Boston to New Orleans, found a place of equal size which surpassed our little mountain city in all the elements of polished and agreeable society.

Elder Graham had just resigned the Chair of Belles-Lettres and History in Kentucky University, which he had filled with such ability that inducements which few men would have resisted were offered to retain him; but he saw such a broad and promising field in the South-West that he resolved to forego comparative ease, honor, and emolument, and to enter upon such a life of toil as few men propose to themselves, simply from a conviction of duty and a desire to be greatly useful. He had taken the position of General Agent for the purpose of permanently endowing Arkansas College, and at the same time expected to do much to extend the influence of the Church of which he was a member; and his eloquence, zeal, and untiring energy, added to his previous success as solicitor for public aid in a work so noble, promised the most gratifying results. Judge Tebbetts was deeply interested and warmly engaged in these designs. The College under my supervision was maintaining its well-earned reputation. We were all about the same age, in the prime of life, had all been successful, had all secured a competency, and were all engaged in a work which had far more reference to the future of others than any present good to ourselves; when the cloud arose which soon overshadowed the land—the dark precursor of that storm which has brought desolation to so many households and woe to so many hearts.

These remarks, kind reader, we have made that you may judge of our opportunities for knowing something of the men and the times of which we write, and which we think qualify us to give, from the abundant material furnished by experience, if a dark, sad, tearful, yet, at the same time, truthful picture of secession in the South-West. While, however, my position and associations afforded me a most favorable field for observation, more than these are necessary to present the truth fully and fairly before the reader's mind—a freedom from prejudice and all the low feelings of the mere partisan, an appreciation of the noble traits of a deceived and misguided people, detestation of the unprincipled leaders, and at the same time sympathy for the suffering masses, are indispensable.

Fifteen of the best years of my life have been spent in the South; my most successful labors in the school-room, the pulpit, and the professor's chair have been bestowed there, and it would be strange if I could easily forget or lightly speak of those whom I have led through the various paths of learning, or have been instrumental in bringing into the fold of Christ. No! the warm welcome I received when I first went there a stranger, the years of unvarying kindness which followed, the happy marriages I have solemnized, the joyful departure of sainted ones that I have witnessed, the warm friendships formed, the strong attachment of pupils, the more sacred ties of religious association, the birth of my children there, and the repose of two of them in its soil, all forbid that I should be the enemy, the maligner of the South. Nor was my sojourn there confined to a single locality; I know something of the coast and islands of the Gulf, have traversed Mississippi from the Louisiana to the Tennessee line, and from the Mississippi River to the Bay of St. Louis; one of my college classmates and intimate friend was the nephew of Jefferson Davis; I resided at one time on the plantation on which was fought the battle of Thompson's Hills; I knew many who have perished in the various battles, from privates to officers of a high grade; I well remember hearing in the State-House at Baton Rouge the stirring eloquence of Louisiana's most-gifted son, Charles Dreux, who fell near Richmond early in the struggle; and these, with a thousand other circumstances crowding upon me as I write, bid me be calm and kind, while faithful and true. Nay! a mist comes over my eyes as the forms of some of the best and most-gifted youth I have ever known rise up to my view from more than one bloody field, where they fell fighting under "a banner with a strange device," while their hearts, O saddest thought! were with the flag and the cause against which they battled. If a man, then, may know his own heart, I feel assured that no malice lurks in mine; that no personal spleen is the secret of this my labor, but that I am animated by a purpose both pure and good—by a desire, not to write a history, but to gather up some precious fragments that would else be lost—to do justice to some noble, because tried, ones, and by these incidents sketch, if not a brilliant panorama, at least some of the bright lights and dark shadows of the war.

The election of Abraham Lincoln threw the whole South into a ferment; every-where men looked into the faces of their fellows and asked what must be done, for truth demands that it be told that the fearful alternative of secession had not suggested itself to the minds of thousands. The convention of border States seemed to promise much, and Arkansas fully expected to be represented there. Conservative men were in favor of trying every thing save the fearful remedy of separation. On the other hand, the advantages of direct trade, the greater security of slave property, the boundless wealth of the South when released from dependence on the North were insisted upon, and when it was intimated that peaceable secession was impossible, it only produced a laugh of scorn; the idea of Northern mechanics, brought up in workshops, unskilled in horsemanship and the use of firearms, endeavoring to cope successfully with those accustomed to the saddle and the use of the rifle from childhood, was not to be mentioned or heard with gravity. The latter class, however, were at first largely in the minority; men who by honorable industry had acquired a competency, and even wealth, thriving mechanics, rising public men, prosperous merchants, and well-to-do farmers were fearful of a change which at best would not bring increased prosperity, and might bring ruin. But men largely indebted at the North, to whom a severance might bring an easy release; planters nominally wealthy, but really bankrupt; broken-down politicians, and such men only as had nothing to lose, whom nothing but a revolution or a rebellion could bring to the surface and give a bad prominence, were in favor of following in the path in which South Carolina had led.

The proof of this is found in the fact that most of the seceding States were hurried out of the Union without even the semblance of the forms of law: Missouri, by the famous Pineville Convention, and Arkansas by a convention of which two-thirds of the members were elected by the votes of Union men—our county, Washington, with the largest voting population in the State, sending the whole delegation, four in number, by a Union vote of from nineteen hundred to twenty-one hundred, out of a voting population of twenty-five hundred, or a majority of from four or five to one. Indeed, this body at its first meeting rejected the ordinance of secession by a two-thirds vote; but on being called together again, under the influence of threats, promises, false telegraphic dispatches, false charges against the Government, and all the appliances which traitors know so well how to use, the fatal measure was carried, and the State hurried into the whirlpool of treason and ruin.

One man alone had the firmness to carry out the pledge he had given to those who sent him there; and though all the arts of flattery and persuasion were tried, he was unyielding; though those who had proved false clamored for his life, he was undismayed; and he is now the loyal Governor of the State whose interests he so boldly refused to betray.

Thousands, it is true, were indignant at the act of the Convention, but the fact that the treasury and arsenal were in the hands of the secessionists, that the power of the Confederacy was pledged to maintain the position the State was forced unjustly to assume, and the significant fact that Arkansas regiments were sent east of the Mississippi, and Texas and Louisiana troops brought into Arkansas, prevented any open resistance on the part of the loyal men of the State. When an individual or a people have determined upon a false step, a plea of justification is never wanting; hence the election of Mr. Lincoln was made the pretext for charging upon the North all manner of intended injustice to the South. Abolition, coercion, negro equality, subjugation became watchwords with the favorers of secession; and when any one ventured to urge that it was unjust to charge upon Mr. Lincoln a policy that he had not as yet indicated, that it would be better to wait for his acts instead of condemning him in advance, the charge of Black Republicanism was the usual retort.

Indeed, so well was the public mind prepared on these matters that, when the President's inaugural was issued, in the eyes of many it contained the obnoxious sentiments above-mentioned; which fact a circumstance, which occurred on the day that it was telegraphed to us, will illustrate. Just after leaving the telegraph office I stepped into a store, where I found quite an excited party discussing the policy presumed to be set forth in the Inaugural; among them was a State Senator from one of the rural districts, who, addressing me, said he supposed "that I was now satisfied, from the President's own words, that he was a favorer of negro equality." To which I replied, "that I did not so read it." "What!" exclaimed he, "does he not quote the language of the Constitution that all men are created free and equal?" In answer to this, I said: "The Constitution contains no such language as that which you have attributed to the President;" which caused a look of astonishment from the bystanders who were of his way of thinking, and regarded him as an oracle, on political matters at least; he then repeated his assertion, upon which I remarked that the language quoted by the President was to be found in the Declaration of Independence. "Well," said he, "it is all the same thing." "With this difference," said I; "that the Constitution has the force of a law, while the other is a declaration of rights, and has no binding force whatever." As there was no reasonable reply possible to this, he began to indulge in a style of remark in which wounded pride and personal spleen were so mingled that I felt that further reply was not only useless, but might also prove injurious; but from that time I knew that the evil eye was upon me.

Soon after the assault upon Sumter I encountered, in the telegraph office, a physician, a man of some influence, then engaged in raising a military company. He charged the North with plunging us into a war destined to produce untold suffering; when I remarked that the South could not justly blame the North for the war, since she had provoked it by striking the first blow, and that we could no more expect the North to submit to such an insult than we could bear a similar one ourselves. On this he flamed out in language most bitter and threatening, intimating that such sentiments would no longer be tolerated, but that popular violence would be employed against those who took the liberty of expressing such views; and this, in the existing state of public feeling, the very worst elements ready for an explosion the moment a spark fell or direction was given to the popular rage, was by no means an idle threat, or to be lightly regarded. In this instance it proved harmless, while the brave, yet misguided, man who gave it utterance had his career soon and suddenly ended by a bullet through the heart in his first battle; and the Senator, though vain and ignorant, but by no means a coward, when I last heard of him, was suffering from a thigh shattered by a Federal ball at Prairie Grove.

CHAPTER II.

PATTING THE TIGER.

Course pursued by Union men—Why we did not leave
at the first outbreak—Scenes in college—Students
enlisting—Fate of my pupils.

THE incidents in the previous chapter were not given to
prove that I was openly and boldly, in public and private, an
uncompromising Union man; like the reed in the storm, with
many others, I had often to bend to the blast. True, whenever
the matter was brought to an issue, I never denied or concealed
my sentiments, but, at the same time, I never made a boast or
parade of them; this, besides being very offensive, was attended
with great danger, and as there may be great bravery in one man
fighting a whole regiment, and yet but little discretion, so there
may be great moral courage, and yet but little prudence in still
further irritating an already unreasoning and infuriated mob.

Still my position was never doubted by friend or foe; if
silent, when to have spoken would perhaps have imperiled life
and at the same time have been of no advantage to the cause
so near my heart, my friends knew very well that in common
with themselves I was "patting the tiger;" seeking to soothe
where I could not successfully resist, while at the same time it
took away from my foes the very pretext they might have
desired for my destruction. Union men in the South, be it
remembered, were not allowed, like disloyal men at the North,
to utter their sentiments with impunity; silence there was criminal, and many lost their lives, not because they had raised either

hand or voice against the leaders of the secession movement, but because they held themselves aloof from the measures of those whom much secession had rendered mad.

The course I pursued, I am satisfied, was that of hundreds of loyal men, though by many carried to a much greater extent; for in thegeneral distrust which reigned, many true men carried their dissimulation—shall I call it?—so far as to deceive not only their enemies, but to cause doubt in the mind of their friends; but the deception and doubt were generally dissipated by finding out that they had been silently converting their property into gold, and then on the first favorable opportunity leaving, not for some more Southern State of the Confederacy, but for one under Lincoln rule; thus indicating where their hearts had ever been. Some who attempted this were stopped and turned back, and their movements afterward closely watched; and all who succeeded in making their escape were bitterly denounced as abolitionists.

The reader may wonder why the writer and his friends did not make their escape as well as others. In the first place, had we done so, these pages would never have been written for lack of the requisite experience; but, as the world would still have revolved in the absence of these records, some other reasons may be deemed necessary for the course we pursued. When the Ordinance of Secession was passed I did not scruple to say that it was equivalent to an act of emancipation; a breaking of the chains it was designed to rivet; of all means the best adapted to secure the result it was intended to avoid. But in common with my friends I never dreamed of the vast proportions which the contest was destined to assume.

Besides this we saw nothing to indicate that our region would be made the seat of war; secure amid our mountains, we thought that the faint murmurs of the strife would reach us from the seaboard and the great rivers, where alone, we thought, it would rage, for our distance from great streams and railways and our comparatively thin settlements were unfavorable to the march and subsistence of a large army. Next came the difficulty of converting our property into money, and, like most men under similar circumstances would have done, we determined to make an effort to save that which had cost us so many years of toil to accumulate. And though the time came when such reasons ceased to have any weight, yet, I suppose, there are none who have secured an agreeable home and enough to make the decline of life free from the fear of want, who would not have felt and made the same effort as we did.

In a word, our homes were dear to us as to others, beautiful and adorned to suit our individual tastes, expecting, as we did, to end our lives there. It was not strange that we should hope that the war would be brief, that it would never come near us, and that with peace there would come again prosperity.

Much more than this had we to bind us there; educational facilities of a high order, acquaintances formed in the best years of our lives, pupils in whom we could not but feel a deep interest, religious ties of no common strength, and last, we all had those little grassy mounds to which often through life memory will go back—the graves of our dead. These all combined to detain us there; and when the time came which gave the assurance that the hopes which led to our stay would never be realized, we were environed by an army which looked upon an attempt to escape as a crime. Then we had no election; stay we must.

Having thus placed before the reader the circumstances necessary to the proper understanding of what follows, I will now attempt a more orderly method, and, by presenting what took place in the College under my charge, may be able to convey some idea of many similar scenes at various institutions through the South. Although I had long been engaged in teaching, I never had a class to which I was so much attached, and of which I felt so proud, as that under my charge during the session of '60–'61. My position brought me in contact with all the students every morning, but the senior students were the special objects of my care; many of them had received instruction from me in the rudiments of classic learning, and now were rapidly bringing those studies to a close. I had given them a fuller course than usual, and they had received unqualified praise from distinguished teachers, one of whom, whose life had been devoted to the instruction of young men, declared that they had not only accomplished more than any class he had ever known, but more than he had deemed possible in the time which they had been employed.

But it was not their highest praise to say that they were devoted and successful students; they were exemplary in their morals, many of them members of the Church, a few of them highly gifted, and while I was greatly attached to them I felt that their attachment was not less to me. Up to the month of March, 1861, the studies had suffered but little interruption; at the close of the first term in January, and on the 22d of February, several addresses were made, mostly in a loyal tone, and some of them in a spirit warmly patriotic; only one or two inclining to the Southern view of affairs. In the Literary Society, too, political matters began to engross considerable attention; sides were taken, with but little bitterness of feeling, however, and in our morning essays and declamations the side espoused by the essayist or speaker was made quite evident. Knowing that the storm could not be averted, I strove in some degree to guide it, and therefore, while I admitted the right of both sides to speak their sentiments; I urged the propriety of regarding each other's convictions, for both might be sincere. And I must confess that the spirit and command of temper exhibited by those young men was remarkable when contrasted with the virulence of the discussions, public and private, which were going on around us.

But recruiting and volunteering began; the feeling among the students on both sides grew warmer; those who were in favor of enlisting began to accuse those who were loyally disposed with a want of courage; the pressure of public sentiment in favor of all young men going into the army began to have its influence, till at length, early in May, a young man, who had ever advocated the Union side, stung, doubtless, by the taunts of cowardice which now began to be heard, closed an address to the students assembled in the college hall for religious and literary exercises, with the words, "Let us die like men!" He was cheered tumultuously, the resolve was taken, the die was cast; they gathered around me, and spoke of the necessity which was upon them, and of their determination to enlist. I bade them meet me yet once more on the next morning; and feeling that parting was inevitable, with tears which were answered by their tears, I uttered my farewell. We parted; and with many of them I shall never meet again till the heavens be no more.

And though all knew my position in regard to the approaching conflict, we parted, as I firmly believe, without an unkind thought on the part even of those who favored the war, with tokens of regret on the faces of all, and with deep sadness on the part of those who, in addition to their regard for me as their instructor and pastor, fully agreed with me on the issues of the hour. To follow the course of those who then were scattered would be a long and sad story, as is evident from what I have learned of the history of a few since that sad day of parting. The youth who led in the movement above recorded was in the Confederate ranks at Wilson's Creek, and came out of the conflict unharmed, although four of his comrades fell by his side; but disease contracted in the camp fastened upon him, and with words of prayer upon his lips he died, and peacefully sleeps his last sleep near the scene of the fearful struggle at Port Hudson. Another, a noble Union boy, had his leg torn away by a cannon-ball at the Pea Ridge fight, and bled to death— dying in a cause he never approved. Some were with Price at Lexington; one was taken prisoner in the rifle-pits at Fort Donelson; the last I heard of another was that he was dying in a hospital at Memphis; another spoke, when I last saw him, of death being preferable to the life he was compelled to lead; and my favorite, if favorite I had when all were loved so well, with

the unsparing conscript law hanging over him, spoke mourn-
fully of the necessity which compelled him to fight without giving him a choice as to the cause in which life must be periled;
another fell at Corinth, and two brothers, side by side, at Iuka;
the leader of those in College in favor of the South, after having passed safely through several battles, was, in my presence,
taken not an unwilling prisoner, and returned to his allegiance;
and of many, very many others I heard not at all, whose fate,
doubtless, has been as varied as that of those I have mentioned.

Thus, doubtless, it was in many portions of the South.
Institutions of learning were broken up, and under the influence of a false pride, or compelled by a relentless conscription
law, those of opposite sentiments fought in the same ranks and
under the same flag. And thus was one of the brightest pages in
my life's history soon sadly blurred with blood and tears. Heaven
grant that the errors of those young men may be forgiven, and
that they may meet in the land of eternal rest and eternal peace!

CHAPTER III.

ROMANCE AND REALITY.

Southern boasting—Hempstead rifles—Waking up—
Wilson's Creek—Price's retreat—Sacking the town.

SOON after the disbanding of our College began what might be termed the romance of the war. Enlistments went on rapidly, and as the secessionists had taken time by the forelock in this matter, by the consolidation of companies which, for months before hostilities broke out, had been on drill, an army sprung up as by magic, and, indeed, in few countries could an army be improvised as rapidly as in the South. Nearly all the young men were perfectly familiar with the use of fire-arms, and the chase had given many perfect mastery of the steed; and in the forests of Louisiana I well remember having seen a noble buck fall beneath the deadly aim of a hunter when deer and horse were in full career.

Such was the contempt for the unwarlike North, that secession orators did not scruple to say that not a thimble-full of blood need be shed in order to secure the independence of the South; and on one occasion, having had an overdose of Southern laudation and Northern depreciation, I proposed, with as much gravity as I could assume, that, since it would be unnecessary to take up arms against such cowards and weaklings as the men of the North, it would be better perhaps to arm the Southern boys with hickory switches, and let them drive our foes from every foot of land that we desired to possess. This, however, was rather too broad a pleasantry, and some very significant looks were exchanged. The ladies, too, caught the war spirit; uniforms, sashes, and banners grew under their active hands; and when the fever was almost at its hight, in marched the "Hempstead Rifles" from the southern portion of the State. Most of them were fine-looking fellows, some of them men of wealth, position, and influence; some of them in former years students of Arkansas College. Their march had been a long one, their drill was perfect, their step and look that of veterans, their arms and uniform all that could be desired; their number, though small, seemed large to people unaccustomed to military spectacles; and when with drums beating and banners flying they marched into the College grounds, and their tents rose as by magic through that hitherto peaceful inclosure, the enthusiasm of the people knew no bounds. A most liberal hospitality was manifested by the citizens; the ladies serenaded their defenders, and the soldiers in gallant style responded with "Advance the Flag of Dixie!" In imagination, Southern independence was achieved, and attentions were lavished upon the soldiers as if victory had already crowned their efforts. Then came the Third Louisiana Infantry, armed with the famous Mississippi rifle, admirable in drill and discipline, perfect in uniforms and accouterments, by far the best regiment in the South-West. These, however, with those before mentioned, were the only Southern troops that I ever saw in any thing like a regular uniform, although on several occasions I saw the armies of Price, M'Culloch, and Hindman. The troops from Louisiana and the southern portion of our State soon formed camps north of us, put picket guards on every road, and all at once we awoke to the fact that we were in the Confederacy, within the Southern lines. The mails stopped, newspapers ceased to be seen, men began to look at the resources of the country, and soon the fact stared every man in the face, that for nearly every necessity, and all the luxuries of life, we had hitherto been dependent on the now hated North. Hardware, school-books, stationery, dry-goods, medicines, implements of agriculture, groceries, carpets, hats, shoes, pins, needles, matches, almanacs, nay, every thing, one might say, were now foreign articles. At home we had cotton without machinery for its manufacture; sugar, with no coffee to sweeten; beef and pork, with a scanty supply of salt to cure it; wheat in a few localities; corn and rice. In all seriousness, I doubt if ever in modern times there was a people so destitute of all that civilization has made necessary for life, and all life's comforts; and the fabulous prices which all such articles soon commanded prove that the picture I have given is not an exaggerated one. In the new zeal for independence, the nature and extent of former dependence had been entirely overlooked, and the effect, when it first flashed on many minds, was to produce blank astonishment.

Blooming Spring blushed into Summer; the first battle of Bull Run was fought with such a result as convinced Southern men of the propriety of the estimate they had placed on Northern valor. Union men, who knew how often Northern courage had been illustrated on fields now historic, were startled at the news and depressed by the general exultation; many who had hitherto hesitated took sides with the victors, less tolerance was shown to those who were true yet timid, and threats were used where argument had failed to convince of the propriety of the Southern movement. Said one to a former warm personal and political friend. "There was a time when one could be a Union man and be honest, but that time is now past." Friends were divided in opinion, few knew whom to trust, not every face showed what was in the heart, and a few were found who said to themselves and to each other, I must either believe that this movement will fail, or must give up my belief in a Providence, my trust in a God. For even then, without the evidences which the struggle has developed of its truth, they saw no attribute in the Divine nature that could array itself in favor of a movement so destitute of justification, so desperate in design, that success itself would have proved most ruinous to those who made the mad attempt.

All at once we were startled by the news, that Gen. Lyon's advance guard, under Sigel, was in Springfield, Mo., about one hundred miles north of us. The Texan Rangers were hurried up to join the infantry already between us and the Federal forces. New levies poured into the various camps daily, and soon an army estimated at from twenty-five thousand to thirty thousand, under Generals M'Culloch, Price, and Pearce, marched against the foe. Notwithstanding M'Culloch's reputation as a wary and watchful chief, his army, outnumbering the enemy three or four to one, was completely surprised by Lyon and Sigel early in the morning of the 10th of August. Indeed, so silent was the march, so perfect the plan of attack, that the first notice they had of an enemy's presence was the shot and shell from the batteries of Totten and Sigel falling into the very heart of their camp. The Federal accounts claim that success would not have been doubtful had the gallant Lyon lived half an hour longer. But the panic that prevailed, and how very nearly the field was lost, could only be told by those whose reports have never seen the light. I have heard persons who were upon the field say, that many were still asleep, many preparing breakfast, and others eating when the enemy's artillery opened upon them. Many fled at the first alarm, but a large army still remained. The contest was long and doubtful, till Lyon, bravely leading a charge in person, fell. The Union forces then withdrew. They charged great excesses upon the pursuing foe; and by the testimony of Southern men who were present, I am satisfied that some of the Federal wounded were deliberately killed on the field after the battle. The victory at Wilson's Creek was a barren one: instead of giving the Confederates a foothold in Missouri, they fell back, and M'Culloch seemed to take a savage pride in desolating the region he was compelled to abandon. The Missouri troops were not satisfied under his command, but were ardently attached to their leader, Gen. Price; and not long after the battle they marched northward, while that portion under M'Culloch fell back into Arkansas.

Our town then became a military post; the Pelican Rifles and Iberville Grays, of the 3d Louisiana Infantry, were quartered in the College building; the Female Seminary was used as an arsenal, and the stables of the Overland Mail Company were seized for the use of the Government. Soon we had a crowd of commissaries and quarter-masters, with their employés; next a flood of Confederate money. Fugitive Missourians found our town a very paradise for horse-dealers; never was trade and traffic so brisk before. Depots for beef and pork were established, and were rapidly filling; food for a large army was collected, mills were pressed for the military service; one thought seemed to animate all, that was—the war. Northward, however, matters were not going on so well; ever and anon trains of wagons filled with negro women and children, the men walking behind, passed on southward, droves of horses and mules in the same direction, and never before, judging from the crowd of emigrants, had Texas seemed so desirable. Rumors began to come in that Price was being forced back; then came couriers in hot haste to M'Culloch for reënforcements. Camps in various parts of the country were broken up, the cavalry left their comfortable quarters on the Arkansas River, and all pressed on toward the Missouri line. A junction of the forces under Price and M'Culloch was effected near Cross Hollows, a position of great natural strength. The Federals were represented as advancing in overwhelming numbers; and as it was thought that a successful stand could not be made, it was decided to fall back to Boston Mountain, and our town was in the line of the retreat.

The reader may hitherto have been in doubt as to the propriety of the title of my book, but we are now entering upon events which I trust will show that it was well chosen, as nearly every incident now will be connected with either the preparations for, or the results of, the battles from which my book takes its name.

The approach of the retreating army was the signal for great activity on the part of army officials, who had charge of the munitions of war and military stores. There was not less on the part of citizens, who expected that the Union army would not be far behind the retreating one. All kinds of vehicles were now in great demand; a span of mules and wagon would bring from six hundred to a thousand dollars; a yoke of steers were as valuable as a pair of fine horses a few weeks before; and happy was the man who had the means of joining in the "hegira" southward. The 20th of February came, and with it some of Price's army, with the intelligence that the rest were coming, and with the next day they came. I was somewhat familiar with the great retreats in history, but never before had I realized the full meaning of the term. Early in the day the Missouri army, which had been marching day and night, constantly harassed by the enemy, made its appearance; the roads were bad, their clothing scanty, their looks dispirited, no music to cheer them, no bright prospects before—it was a practical picture of secession; and O how sadly did the Missouri troops *secede* from their beloved State! thousands of them, alas, never to return! One of the officers, the Judge Advocate of Price's army, stopped awhile at my house, and wept like a child at the thought of leaving home and country behind. There were many others, who complained bitterly because M'Culloch had not come to their aid, to enable them to make a stand on their own soil against the foe now eagerly pressing upon their rear.

The officers of the commissary and quarter-master's department, unable to remove their stores, threw open the various depots to the soldiers and citizens; the permission thus granted was construed into a general license to plunder, and pillage soon became the order of the day. An officer, fearing the effects of liquor upon a wearied, pursued, and reckless soldiery, took the precaution to burst in the heads of a number of barrels of whisky, which constituted a portion of the army stores, and the cellar was soon several inches deep with the precious fluid. By some means the place was discovered, and scores drank the filthy puddle which the spilled liquor had made. Private stores were broken open, and every one helped himself to whatever suited him; and as regiment after regiment poured in to swell the tide of waste and robbery, the scene became one of riot and unrestrained plunder.

And yet, strange to say, this was not in an enemy's country; these men claimed to be the defenders of the very people they were despoiling; and at that very moment the men of Arkansas were acting as rear guard to this very army, engaged, hundreds of them, as I have just stated. Passing among them as I did while thus employed, so general had the work of destruction and plunder become, that it was almost impossible to find a single soldier who did not possess some evidence of being carried away by the spirit of the hour. Here was one with a cigar box half filled with sugar, another with a pair of lady's gaiters sticking out of his pocket; this had a pair of baby's shoes, that, some fine lace; artificial flowers adorned the caps of some; while jars of pickles, tin cups full of molasses, tape, calico, school-books, letters, law papers, sheets of tin plate, in fact nearly every article known to traffic might have been seen in that motley throng. Indeed, any one could see at a glance that the greater part of them had taken articles for which they had no use whatever. Some contented themselves with what really belonged to them—the army stores; and many a wagon filled with fine quarters of beef was hastily unloaded in the street, to be replaced by bacon, immense piles of which had been collected for the use of the various camps in the vicinity. Whole companies would march out of town, each man with a ham, shoulder, or side of bacon on his bayonet, and no one could complain of them for thus wishing to change their camp fare; but what could the others want with fine articles of ladies' wear, and, as I noticed in one case, a thermometer? Officers threatened, cursed, called them thieves, made appeals to their manliness and State pride, and to the fact that they were among those battling in the same cause; but all in vain; stealing had become a kind of recreation, and they would steal. Gen. Price himself strove to check the disorder which I have attempted faintly to describe, but for once his commands were powerless, and the work of ruin went on.

The troops encamped for the night south of us, but many of the officers remained in town; nearly every house was filled; they claimed to be our friends, had long been standing between us and danger, and promised soon to rid our State of the pursuing foe. Their retreat, they said, was only a piece of strategy; they wished to draw the army of Gen. Curtis from its supplies, and beyond the reach of reënforcements; they would get them down to the Boston Mountains, and see that they never returned. Among those that I best remember were Gen. Rains, for once sober and most gentlemanly in his manners; Major Sevier, who shed tears at being thus made "an exile from home;" Churchill Clarke, said to be the best artillerist in Price's army; Emmett M'Donald, who indeed looked and talked like the brave soldier that he was; and Ben. M'Culloch, meditating doubtless upon the dark deeds that the morrow would bring. The night was a long and anxious one; how could it be otherwise, with the rear guard of a fleeing army with us and the pursuers near? All the roads southward were thronged with fugitives; in town were a few who looked for deliverance from the North—those who had suffered and hoped in silence; who had prayed and waited, and now felt that it had not been in vain.

CHAPTER IV.

BURNING THE TOWN.

Among the bombshells—A critical moment—A cavalry
charge—Under the old flag again—A sad incident.

THE next morning dawned, and in haste the officers of the
retreating army departed. But soon bands of Cavalry, by order
of Gen. M'Culloch, dashed into town and began firing the
buildings which had been used for military purposes; some of
them contained large quantities of beef and bacon, which soon
added violence to the flames. Then the large stables, once the
property of the Overland Mail Company, were destroyed; the
steam mill, which had been furnishing the rebel army ten thousand pounds of flour per day, was consumed; and, as we gazed
on the clouds of smoke pierced here and there by tongues of
flame, we felt that the fate of our beautiful mountain city was
sealed.

The worst, however, had not yet come. About fifty yards
from my residence was a large and beautiful structure, in the
days of peace a Female College, but latterly used as a military
arsenal and cartridge manufactory. The ammunition had been
removed, with the exception of a large quantity of condemned
bombshells—the fuses imperfect, but the shells charged with
the elements of destruction. A soldier, lately one of our citizens,
rode up to this building, dismounted, and just when entering
was addressed by some persons living near, and informed them
that he was sent to destroy it; but he evidently had little taste
for the deed. The danger to the women and children in the

dwellings near, from the explosion of the shells in the building, was pointed out to him, and though it involved disobedience of orders, he declared he would do no such deed, remounted and rode off. Scarcely was he out of sight, when a few horsemen galloped up, entered the building, and began to make preparation for burning it by pouring turpentine on the floors and between the ceilings; permission was asked to remove the bombshells, but they refused; the torch was applied, and the flames spread so rapidly that the occupants of the next building had scarcely time to save their trunks and some bedding, before that was also on fire. My own house was now in great danger, and we began to remove what we deemed most valuable; but before we had succeeded to any great extent, the fire reached the bombshells; a terrific explosion took place, not less than twenty bursting at once, scattering the deadly fragments in a hundred directions. Sending away the children to a place of safety, we still strove to save some of our effects from my residence, to which the fire had now reached. We were soon compelled, however, to desist by another volley of bursting shells, loud as a park of artillery, which was heard miles away, and gave rise to the impression that the advance guard of the Union army had come up and were shelling the town. As the attempt to save any thing now seemed hopeless, and to remain in the vicinity was fraught with danger from the still bursting shells, the smoke almost blinding us, and the flames coming still nearer, I took my wife by the hand and strove to lead her away from the danger which threatened. And yet it was rather sad thus to leave the accumulation of years, library, letters, and mementos of friends, all behind; but life was in the other scale, and I urged that we should leave; she replied that the shells must have nearly all burst, and that we must make one more effort to save our home. My friend Graham having just arrived, and gained the roof of the burning dwelling, we made another attempt and subdued the flames.

Although fragments of the shells came alarmingly near several persons, fortunately no one was injured, and by noon Judge

Tebbetts, Elder Graham, and myself were standing sadly contemplating the ruins of what had once been the pride and ornament of our town. While thus engaged, some mounted Confederate soldiers rode up and inquired the reason of such destruction. Graham began the story of M'Culloch's vandalism; he was greatly excited, his eyes flashed, the veins of his neck and forehead seemed ready to burst, there was an indignant flush upon his cheek, and at last, with both hands lifted up, said: "God has rained down fire from heaven on better men than those that did this!" It was a critical moment; the rebels had rifles in their hands, and, had they possessed the spirit of their unscrupulous leader, might have used them. I laid my hand on his arm, enjoined silence by a look, turned the conversation; and as the men had not as yet seen the fitness of their leader's policy in destroying their own towns, they soon rode off in the direction of the army.

From a distance M'Culloch beheld the ruin, the causeless and unnecessary ruin of which he was the author; and when appealed to in behalf of those whose homes were endangered by the fires kindled by his orders, and asked to save Southern women and children from being rendered homeless—from the consideration, too, that he had enjoyed the hospitality of some of those homes at the hands of those who favored the Southern cause—he replied in a manner most brutal, as I learned from the chaplain of one of the Texas regiments under his command, who himself made the request for the protection of women, children, and private property. The few citizens who remained could do little toward arresting the progress of fires in so many different places at the same time; and when night fell a great portion of our town was a smoldering ruin. Another day passed, one of strange quiet; one army had swept by in hurried retreat, the other we felt assured would soon appear in pursuit. Most of the men who favored the Southern cause had left, and to nearly all who remained the approach of the Union army meant deliverance. Night came, and southward the camp-fires of the armies

of Price and M'Culloch could be seen, while to the northern
sky a glow like that of the Aurora Borealis was given by those
of the Federal soldiery. With the next dawn came the report of
the advance of the men of the North; the heavy pickets, pressed
back by the advancing enemy, rode slowly by, and soon in hot
haste came a scouting party who had been watching the movements of the pursuing foe. In answer to our inquiries they said
the "Feds" were rapidly coming; and, indeed, they were with the
swiftness and fury of a storm. The last of the rebel pickets were
but a few hundred yards north of my residence, watching with
deep interest a few gleaming points of steel on the wooded hill
opposite; soon a line of blue wound down the hill-side, the
pickets turned their horses' heads southward; there was a clat-
ter of hoofs, a flashing of sabers, a wild and fierce hurrah; ringing shots from revolvers, men fleeing for life, men and steeds in
the chase both seemingly animated by the same spirit of destruction; in a word, the most exciting of military spectacles; a cavalry charge had been made past my door. Within a few moments
men had been slain and wounded, prisoners taken, and our town
was in possession of the advance guard of the Union army.

And now they streamed in on every side; the whole country seemed alive with mounted men. A loud shout was heard
on the public square; we turned our eyes in that direction, and
a splendid banner, made when the Union sentiment ran high,
but which for months had been concealed, was floating from
the flagstaff on the courthouse, and we were once more under
the Stripes and Stars. Strange that an emblem should have such
power over the human soul! and yet the first sight of the ocean
or the down-rushing flood of Niagara did not waken such emotions as the waving folds of that banner of the free. Carefully
had it been concealed, and faithfully preserved when its possession would have been deemed a high crime if discovered. A
few eyes had been permitted to look upon it in secret during the
dark days; the tones of the voice were low when it was mentioned; on one occasion a Confederate officer had only a

mattress between him and that flag; but now it was flung out once more by loyal hands to the free air, hailed with almost frantic delight by loyal voices, stretched to its utmost tension by a strong breeze; every stripe distinct, every star visible; the old flag, the joy of every loyal heart! Scorn and contumely had been heaped upon it; to mention it, save in condemnation, a crime; its place usurped by another banner, but the day of its triumph had come at last.

Soon the main body of troops, under General Asboth, rode into town. Their appearance, when contrasted with that of the legions of Price, who preceded them, was magnificent; and, indeed, apart from any comparison, they were a noble body of men. They were mostly from Iowa and Illinois; under a chief who had seen service in Europe, and who looked more like a soldier than any of the hastily-improvised Generals who were with the army whose retreat we had just witnessed. The Union ladies warmly and gladly saluted the flag which was borne at the head of the column, and my wife was the first, from the balcony of our dwelling, to wave and shout a welcome. An officer observing her, while thus greeting the banner, called out, "Where are you from?" "Massachusetts," was the reply. "Ah," cried he, "I thought so! I am from that State myself." The house of Judge Tebbetts, opposite mine, was chosen as Head-Quarters, and we all felt glad in the thought that we should never again be left among our enemies, but that they would press on and stand between us and danger. Soon I walked down to the public square, and there saw a bloody saddle—the first blood of the war that I had seen; it was the blood of one of the rebel pickets; and soon I saw the man himself, and aided the surgeon while attending to his ghastly wound; and though there were some secessionists still remaining, it was the hands of loyal people that ministered to him during the few days that he lived, and gave him decent burial when he died.

After remaining two or three days we were informed that the troops with us were to fall back forthwith to the main body.

This was sad news to us; we had welcomed them as friends; jealous eyes had marked the mutual trust which had been manifested, and the protection we had enjoyed, and if our position had ever been doubtful it was so no longer. To remain was now dangerous, and to leave was scarcely less so, as the roads were beset by roving bands which rendered travel next to impossible. Our military friends told us that the army would doubtless soon move southward, and we decided to remain. Scarcely, however, had they left before the Southern army gave tokens of moving northward, to drive back the army by which Price had been forced from Missouri into Arkansas; and as this movement resulted in the hard-fought battle of Pea Ridge, we will introduce an episode or two of some interest before entering upon an account of that now historic field. One of these may serve to show how Union men treated Southern soldiers when forsaken by their friends; the other, how Southern soldiers, on many occasions, treated Union men. Perhaps each case may be a representative one.

As the Confederate army was retreating, as before mentioned, one of M'Culloch's men, of Mitchell's regiment, unable to march any longer, went into a negro cabin in the edge of town, and sank exhausted on the floor; the occupants rendered him all the assistance in their power, but his disease was beyond the reach of the simple means in their possession. I was informed of his condition, and had him removed to a vacant house, and installed in a good room with bed, fire, medicine, and nurse. Soon his symptoms became less violent, and great hopes were entertained of his recovery. But one night, while the Federals held the town, he got up and asked to go out; and to the horror of the nurse, as soon as he got into the yard, he uttered a yell, and, under the influence of the delirium of fever, ran howling into the woods. This, too, without coat, hat, or shoes, on a Winter night. Word was brought to me, and soon, with others, I hastened to the place, but every sound had died away, and, though we searched long and well, no trace of the fugitive could be found. My feelings were beyond description—to think of a human being, a man, a brother, under the influence of a raging fever, half-dressed, roaming through the woods on a Winter night, surpassed all I had ever conceived of the horrible.

At daylight our search was resumed, but without success, and little doubt was entertained that he had perished from exposure. But soon after sunrise I saw one of the Federal pickets passing my door with the escaped patient a prisoner. His eyes were wild and glaring, and his cheeks red as blood with the fever flush. He supported his steps with a large ragged branch of a tree; his countenance expressed the greatest terror, and he presented at once the strangest and saddest sight I had ever beheld. I approached the soldier, who told me that he came near the picket guard, shouting and screaming, about the middle of the night; that they had taken him up, and he was now taking him to Head-Quarters to have him disposed of. I asked if he could not see that he was delirious and almost dying, and asked him to give him up to me; he admitted all I said, but replied that he had no discretion in the matter, and must take him to the officer of the guard. I then asked him to delay a moment; and running to Head-Quarters, briefly stated the case to General Asboth, who sent an aid with me to order his release, if the case was such as I stated. As soon as he saw him the necessary order was given, and I led him into my house. Under our care he rallied a little; Reason once or twice resumed her sway, and during one of his lucid intervals he offered up a most fervent, touching, and appropriate prayer, in which he named a number of his relatives whose welfare was nearest his heart; but the shock had been too severe, and though we watched him day and night for four weeks, and left nothing undone that could minister to his comfort, he died, and was buried decently and tenderly by stranger-hands. The very day he died I was taken down with the same disease, and lay dangerously ill for weeks. His only effects were a few letters which indicated the residence of his parents and young wife, and a Methodist hymn-book.

His regiment was near our town once and again, but no inquiry was ever made for him; the entire stoppage of the mails made it impossible to inform his friends of his sad fate; and I write it deliberately, when I say that this is only one of very many cases which have proved to me that there was in the Southern army the greatest recklessness of human life—hundreds, like him, were left by the wayside to perish; no inquiries were made as to their fate, and of thousands the story how they died will never be told. Nor was this the solitary instance in which Union men forgot the rebel in the man. I never knew them to with-hold aid when needed, and it was often proffered and accepted when secessionists saw, and yet put forth no hand to relieve, the sufferings of their brethren.

CHAPTER V.

IN PRISON.

Judge Tebbetts arrested—My own narrow escape—A Union woman's trials—Tebbetts before M'Culloch—A false friend—A true friend—The presentiment—The trial and release.

OUR severest trial was now at hand: the three friends whose hearts had been as the heart of one man, were about to be severed, and that, too, under circumstances calculated to give rise to the deepest anxiety and the most fearful forebodings. Scarcely a day had passed without seeing each other; we knew that we were objects of suspicion, and, save when with each other, our words and very looks had to be guarded; indeed, we knew by experience what it was to live during a "reign of terror."

Gen. M'Culloch soon learned that the troops under Gen. Asboth had fallen back, and determined to wreak his vengeance upon the Union men who had failed to flee with his retreating army, and who were speedily reported to him as having welcomed the invaders. Most prominent among these was Judge Tebbetts, at whose house the flag was found which floated in triumph for a few days, and where Gen. Asboth made his Head-Quarters. Those who informed upon him, and thus placed his life in peril, might have said with truth, that there was a dying Confederate soldier under his roof receiving the kindness and care which secessionists had failed to proffer; and that the persons and property of many fared much better than would have been the case had his good word been wanting. Indeed, he spoke well in every case where it was possible—where he could not speak well he spoke not at all; nay, in some instances, he spoke well of those whose conduct afterward proved that they were unable to appreciate his kindness. All this, and more, might have been told M'Culloch, but would scarcely have had any influence with the coarse, brutal, and profane Texan. As it was, the day after Gen. Asboth's departure, two or three troopers dismounted at his door, and in a few minutes rode with him a prisoner between them toward the Southern camp.

The blow fell with stunning effect upon his friends; their very friendship, if known, would endanger them without benefiting him, and this made it intolerable; to know the peril of one for whom we would have ventured even life itself, and yet to know that the effort would be in vain, was a trial which we felt to be by far the greatest that we had been called upon to undergo. Indeed, the writer himself narrowly escaped the same fate: some soldiers on a similar errand rode up to my door, and but for my wife's presence of mind I should doubtless have shared the fortunes of my friend. When they rode up I had not been absent from the house many minutes, and expecting to return shortly had not mentioned where I was going. They asked my wife if I was at home; she replied I was not. Where had I gone? She did not know. When would I return? She was unable to say. These and similar questions, met by similar answers, gave them no clew as to where I was; and as Federal scouts were riding all over the country, they thought it neither prudent to wait nor to search for me. I returned but a few minutes after their departure, and fearing their return betook myself to a place of safety; and it was well that I did so, for again they came; and when, after several days' absence, I was about to come home, a messenger reached me in my place of security and secrecy, telling me not to venture back, as M'Culloch's men had been in search of me the third time. O! what nights were those upon that mountain-top; what long and anxious days among the cliffs and caverns of the rocks, hiding like a criminal, hourly in danger of being hunted like a wild-beast, my only crime, attachment to the Government under which I had enjoyed so many blessings, and which never had inflicted on me a single wrong.

But to return. After the arrest of my friend, I ran over to his house, expecting to find his wife overcome with grief at the sudden calamity which had fallen upon her. I knew something of her deep and strong attachment; I had often witnessed her anxiety when he had in other days met with any unexpected delay; and now that he was thus rudely separated, and on his way, as we little doubted, to a violent death, how deep must be her anguish? But no; she shed not a tear, she uttered no cry, that hour had made her as firm and self-reliant as ever was Roman matron or Spartan wife; she felt the deep wrong inflicted upon her husband, she knew the cause for which he was suffering, and she acted as the noble wife of a noble man who was suffering in a noble cause.

Consulting my feelings, only, I made offer of my services to go to the Southern camp, and endeavor to serve her husband, or learn his probable fate; she kindly but firmly replied, "No, you can not serve him; your views and principles are the same; you would endanger yourself and could do him no service—do not go." This was true, I felt it to be so; and the fact that soldiers were soon on my track to arrest me, proved that her woman's instinct was right. Sometimes during her husband's imprisonment I feared the struggle would be too much for her; the firm resolve of that face, once all gentleness, and the fixed look, nay, almost glare of those eyes, once so full of tenderness as they looked upon husband and children, seemed at times almost unnatural; but never did she abate her loftiness of demeanor, which was truly queenly during all the terrible ordeal through which she was called to pass. I remember on one occasion, soon after her husband's arrest, that the Provost Marshal of our town, a Western man, too, traitor alike to his country and

State, and for that reason an object of contempt, came to her house and demanded her blankets and carpets for the use of the Confederate army; she made no complaint, expressed no surprise, did not even show the contempt she felt for his course, but bore herself as loftily as if conferring a favor instead of obeying a coarse and unlawful command. She ordered her carpets to be taken up, dusted, folded, and delivered to him, without betraying by a word or look a sense of the indignity put upon her. Even the children caught in a measure the spirit of the mother; the father was in a prison—that they felt to be no disgrace—in peril, yet for no crime, unless it were a crime to be "faithful among the faithless;" and in after years their father's imprisonment will bring the flush to their cheeks, but it will not be the flush of shame. I have dwelt on this from the conviction that I have, in describing one, been depicting many true-hearted Union women, who, amid disaster to the cause and the danger of those they loved, proved themselves worthy of the blessings they had long enjoyed, and which, when they could do nothing else, they prayed might long be the heritage of their children; and their prayers have been heard.

But to return to the husband and father. He was arrested about four in the afternoon, and hurried off in the direction of Boston Mountain, where the Southern army was encamped. About twelve miles from Fayetteville the party reached the lines, and there the prisoner was met by some officers of the Arkansas troops, by whom he was well known, who expressed surprise and regret at seeing him in that condition, and offered to accompany him to Head-Quarters and procure his release. M'Culloch, however, rudely refused to see them, and directed the guard to conduct the prisoner to Col. Hebert, with the order to "keep the d—d scoundrel under double guard, safe for hanging." The Colonel expressed regret at his misfortune, but was obliged to respect the orders of his chief, and the night was passed under guard in the midst of an army frantic with rage at being driven back, and ready to inflict summary vengeance on any one suspected of loyalty. The night was bitter cold; the camp-fires were visible for miles around. The prisoner had ample time to look into his own heart; and, as he looked up to the quiet stars, he felt that he could thank God that his heart was true to the flag which the stars bedecked, and for which he now felt the stripes of suffering. The gleam of bayonets was before his eyes, the regular tread of the guard struck his ears, forebodings most fearful of the morrow crowded upon his mind, but amid all this his heart reproached him not, for his, he felt, was not a traitor's heart, and suffering for the right scarcely seemed suffering. Morning came; the news had spread through the camp that a "Union traitor" had been caught, and, as he was escorted to Head-Quarters, the cries "shoot him!" "hang him!" were heard on every side; and thus amid insults and threats—the guards accelerating his pace occasionally by the application of their bayonets—he was brought into the presence of M'Culloch and a portion of his staff.

His first salutation was, "Well, you are here, d—n you!" "Yes," was the reply; "what are the charges against me?" "You will find that out soon enough," he replied, with his usual, or rather habitual oath. "How long have you been in Arkansas?" "Nearly a quarter of a century." "Are you a native of the South?" "No, I was born in New Hampshire." "A d—d Yankee; I thought so." After venting his spleen in his usual style, which was both coarse and profane, he informed him that the charges were— that he had remained in Fayetteville after its evacuation by the Southern army; that he had entertained Gen. Asboth and staff; had presented the Federals with a United States flag; had made a speech on the occasion; that he was a d—d traitor to the South; that he might prepare for the worst, as he would leave nothing undone to have him hung, and that the more prominent the man the better would be the example; that he was then too much occupied, as he was just about to move on the enemy, but that when he returned he would see that he got his deserts.

The rage of the malignant and uncivilized creature had hitherto failed to provoke any reply, but at last, prisoner as he was, his New England blood was stirred, and, with a look full as bold as that of his persecutor, and snapping his fingers in his face, he said: "Ben M'Culloch, do your worst!"

He was then sent to Fort Smith till the army should return, and reached there the same night, was thrust into a cell, and the light of the next morning came to him through the bars of a prison. The commander of the post was Major G. W. Clarke, an old acquaintance of the prisoner, one, too, whom he had often befriended in such a way as to establish such a claim upon his gratitude as no true man would have failed to acknowledge. Their positions were now changed, but not a look or word of sympathy indicated the recollection of former favors; but, on the contrary, his first words were an insult. "Tebbetts," said he, "I am sorry I can't offer you my hand." "I don't wish to take your hand," said the prisoner; "and you might have delayed your apology till I offered mine." He was then informed that an order had been issued suspending the writ of *habeas corpus*, and that he need not attempt an appeal to the civil authorities. The newspapers issued bulletins magnifying the causes of his arrest; rumor spread the gravest charges against him; bitter was the feeling, and great the exultation at the capture of an enemy so dangerous to the South.

The solitude of his prison gave ample opportunity for reflection; the excited state of public feeling, and the threat of the rebel General hanging over him led him to anticipate the worst; indeed, he made up his mind that his end was near, and he experienced the feelings of one upon whom sentence had been passed, and calmly determined to meet his fate in such a manner as not to cause his children to blush for their father. The cause for which he was suffering and for which he expected to lay down his life was as dear to him as ever, and he had no misgivings as to the final result; it was the old story of the martyrs over again—he was sustained by a consciousness of the purity of his motives, and learned by experience that in a just cause one could suffer and be strong.

The news of his arrest was spread all over the South; a friend in Texas heard that his execution was soon to take place, and leaving all his property which he had removed there for safety, he traveled day and night till he reached Fort Smith, in the hope of being of some service to him. He was a Missourian, had been in the Confederate service, was personally known to, and had great influence with, Gen. Price; to use that influence and save a friend, if possible, was his only motive, and the world ought to know that his name is Joe Davis, of Henry county, Missouri; an honest and a true man, who, misguided though he had been, never deserted a friend.

Some ladies, who had known him in happier times, sent food and conveniences for his place of confinement; some sent flowers, some assurances of their earnest prayers for his safety. A few men in the community began to think it hard that a man, guilty of no crime, should be imprisoned at the will of a military despot; and through a faithful negro—whom he after- ward emancipated—who had volunteered to pass through the Southern lines to get news of his master to carry back to his family, he learned that there was quite a change of public sen- timent in his favor. Charges of the most extravagant character had been circulated against him, and when the truth came out, not only that they were false, but that he had befriended even rebels when sick and wounded, the change became so great that he became an object of sympathy, and complaints began to be uttered against the General who had ordered his arrest. In the mean time M'Culloch had made an advance against the army under Gen. Curtis, and news came that the conflict at Pea Ridge had begun. No fears were entertained as to the result, as the Southern troops outnumbered the Federals four to one.

Judge Tebbetts was sitting alone in his prison, thinking how his own fate was linked with the fortunes of the battle then in progress; his thoughts had assumed a somber hue as he thought of home, of wife and children, and despondence, greater than he had ever before experienced, took possession of him. While thus occupied in fancies and reflections, the saddest he had ever known, all at once the thought, like an inspiration, flashed upon his mind, Why are you doubtful and despairing? your deliverance has been wrought out—Ben M'Culloch is dead. Few men have less superstition in their composition than he, and yet at that moment he felt as fully assured of the death of the rebel chieftain as he did a few days after when his body was brought into Fort Smith. Singular as it may seem, no one in Fort Smith had even thought of such an event; the news from the battle-field was encouraging, all were fully anticipating a most decisive victory, and yet this prisoner *knew*—I know of no other word that will express the strength of his conviction—that the day was lost, and that M'Culloch was dead; nay, more, that as the result of these events his release was certain. From deep despondency he passed into a state of joy and assurance that all would be well; and though he strove to analyze his own feelings, and to undermine the foundations of his new and strange joy, reasoning against the unreasonableness of his convictions, he found that he could not impair their strength. To him it was, to all intents and purposes, a revelation. And when, some time after, a courier from the battle-field dashed into the fort, and the commandant rushed into his room, crying out, "All is lost! we are defeated, thrown into utter rout, M'Culloch is killed, our army in full flight!" it caused no surprise; he merely said: "Ah, indeed!" It was no news to him; he knew it before.

My friend was no visionary, few men indeed less so; a lawyer by profession, skilled above most of his class in detecting weak points in evidence, requiring more and clearer testimony than most men, he no more doubted than he did his own existence that the battle of Pea Ridge was lost, and M'Culloch slain, before any message or testimony to that effect had been received. Soon after, the body of the fallen General was brought to Fort Smith, and the fatal wound examined. He was shot through the breast, the ball passing entirely through the body, and fell from his clothes when he was undressed. The ball was shown by Major Brown, of M'Culloch's staff, to Judge Tebbetts; and though he mused upon the influence which that small globe of lead that he held in his own hands had upon his own fate, and which was far more precious, lead that it was, than one of gold or diamond could be, yet even then he felt not a stronger conviction of the death of his relentless enemy, than he did in the solitude of his prison before human voice had uttered in his hearing the words, Ben M'Culloch is dead. We may call it strange, mysterious, unaccountable; but it is true.

Soon the beaten army fell back on Fort Smith, and Judge Tebbetts addressed a letter to Van Dorn, who had assumed command but a few days before the battle, demanding a trial, which was granted, and the prisoner was brought before Major Sevier, Judge Advocate of Price's Division. The principal charges were, that he had in his possession a United States flag, and that he had refused to receive Confederate money. Others far more grievous, but false, had been made, but no witnesses appeared to prove them. He admitted the first charge, which the Judge Advocate declared to be no crime; said he, there is a United States flag at my house in Missouri, and I used to think it a very good flag too. On the second charge, he asked the Judge Advocate if it was not his right if he chose to refuse to take Confederate money; the reply was, most certainly; he then stated that he had never refused to take it in payment of any debt due him, and that he had even taken it for property for which he had paid gold; this he proved by several witnesses. The charges were declared to be not sustained; several instances of kindness extended by the accused to Southern men were volunteered, and the order was given for an honorable discharge. The truth is, though a Union man, who never faltered for a moment, he performed many kind offices for sick, wounded, and suffering Southern men, not because they were rebels, but men, and he did not lose his reward. Had Ben M'Culloch lived, how different, doubtless, would have been the result! but there is a God above.

CHAPTER VI.

BATTLE OF PEA RIDGE.

The Confederates advance—They meet Sigel—Death of
M'Culloch and M'Intosh—News from the field—Flight of
the army southward—The sharp-shooter.

BUT to resume the thread of our narrative. The living tide
which had swept through our town on its way to the Boston
Mountains began to flow back. Van Dorn had arrived to take the
command of all the forces in that region. We heard the salutes
which welcomed his arrival, and about the same time there came
the first news from Fort Donelson; but how different from the
reality: it was represented as an unmitigated disaster to the Union
cause; twenty thousand prisoners had been taken, and the
Confederate cavalry were in hot pursuit of the remnant of the
fleeing host. Bulletins to this effect were circulated through the
camp, and all felt certain that a similar fate soon awaited the
little army of Gen. Curtis, then encamped in the vicinity of the
now famous field of Pea Ridge; and, though much has been written concerning this—one of the most important and stoutly-
contested battles of the war—yet I am bold to say that the story
of that field has not yet been told. In the official reports of Gen.
Curtis and his division commanders, the occurrences of the three
eventful days are clearly and modestly set forth; but neither he
nor they were aware of the utter rout of the enemy, from the fact
that they had no large body of cavalry to follow up the victory.
As it was, it was decisive; but even an unmilitary eye like my
own, witnessing the disorderly, hasty, and confused flight of that

broken and shattered army, could see that a few regiments of fresh cavalry could have captured prisoners by the regiment—as will appear in the sequel.

Gen. Curtis estimates the forces he met and vanquished at about thirty thousand, three times the number of his own little but brave band; but the Southern men themselves claimed a much larger force: by most it was placed at from forty to forty-five thousand, by some at over fifty thousand; and from the number of the regiments, nearly all of them full, and from the appearance of the troops and the time it took them to pass, I think forty thousand rather inside than beyond the real number. In Price's army were the divisions of Rains, Slack, and Frost. M'Culloch had a large army before the retreat from Cross Hollows, and many newly-raised regiments were said to have joined him at Boston Mountain; and to these must be added the Indian Brigade under Gen. Pike.

Most of these troops passed through our town on the 3d and 4th of March, the rear guard remaining all the last night, a night not soon to be forgotten by me, as it witnessed the conflagration of our beautiful College building, the scene of so many useful and pleasant hours. Having escaped the torch during the retreat of Price and M'Culloch, some ten days before, we had hoped that it would be spared, but we were doomed to disappointment; the night was clear and cloudless, not a breath of air was stirring, and, as the smoke curled skyward in the calm of midnight, this shrine of learning, the abode of peace, fell a sacrifice to the fierce spirit of war and destruction. The quiet which reigned after the army had passed northward was soon broken by the roar of artillery, which told that the battle had begun; this firing took place near Bentonville, where Van Dorn, in his report of the battle, says that he found Sigel posted with a force of seven thousand strong. The truth is that Sigel was there, but with not quite as many hundreds as he was reputed to have thousands; with this small yet determined band he kept fighting and retreating: checking the advance of the enemy by a furious and well-directed artillery fire, he would retreat; make another stand, and repeated the process till he joined the main body, about twelve miles from where the battle began; and I have no doubt but the desperate fighting, and the severe loss inflicted upon the enemy during that well-conducted retreat, was well calculated to create and keep up the impression that Sigel had seven thousand instead of but six hundred men.

This falling back in the face of an overwhelming force was called a retreat of all the Federal forces; and we soon got news that the invading army was in full flight for Missouri, and then that it had been overtaken and surrounded. At this juncture our feelings were not of the most agreeable character. One of our number—and the number of Union men at that time was very few—was in a prison, which he and his best friends feared would soon be exchanged for a more dreadful fate. The secessionists were triumphant; nothing less than the capture of Gen. Curtis's command would satisfy them, and the news constantly coming in seemed to indicate that their wishes would be gratified.

Our news, be it remembered, however, was from the Southern side alone; we knew nothing of the splendid strategy of Sigel, the truly chivalrous deeds of Asboth, the unflagging courage and endurance of Carr, Davis, and, indeed, of every man in those terrible three days, for every man there did his duty. How cheering to us would have been the knowledge of the calm self-reliance of Curtis, who, though surrounded, as he knew, by a vastly-superior foe, abated neither heart nor hope, having come to fight, not to surrender! Thus passed Thursday and Friday: on Saturday morning the news was not so favorable for the exultant expectants of a triumph before which all others were to pale; the contest was said to be fearful, the slaughter on both sides immense; still the advantage was with the South; Price had got between the enemy and Missouri, and all hope of escape was cut off, the invaders would never return save as exchanged prisoners. About ten in the morning came the news of the charge made by the mounted Texan regiments, under M'Culloch and M'Intosh, upon the Federal batteries; the carnage was fearful, and an officer of distinction on the Southern side was reported killed; no one conjectured who it could be. Then the report came that a carriage was coming containing a wounded officer; and one of those who had just returned from the battle-field said: "It is true, gentlemen, that a carriage is coming, but the officer in it, be he whom he may, is dead, for I helped to lift him into it; his face was covered, I did not know him, but that he is dead I know." Soon the carriage came in sight; I went across the square to inquire whose body it contained, and was informed that it was a wounded man belonging to one of the Texan regiments. I had seen enough of the treatment of common soldiers to know that this could not be so; the carriage kept on toward Fort Smith, and we soon learned that it contained the body of the famous Ben M'Culloch.

This was unexpected and startling, matters began to wear a serious aspect; and, just after nightfall, hearing a wagon from the direction of the battle-ground passing my door, I went out to make some inquiries, and found that it contained the body of Gen. James M'Intosh, who fell nearly at the same time with M'Culloch.

The body was taken into the house of an acquaintance of mine; I entered, and there he lay, cold and stark, just as he was taken from the spot where he fell; a military overcoat covering his person, and the dead forest leaves still clinging to it. His wound had not been examined; I aided in opening his vest and undergarments, and soon found that the ball had passed through his body, near, if not through, the heart. Some officers of the 3d Louisiana—some of them wounded—came with the body; their regiment, the best in Van Dorn's army, had suffered severely; the colonel, who was commander of a brigade of infantry, the major, and several other officers had been captured, and the losses were reported as heavy; indeed, both regiment and brigade were without commanders, all fitted for such positions being wounded or prisoners. Returning home from the sad scene I heard the sound of a horse's feet coming down the road from the battle-field; soon horse and rider came into view, both evidently much jaded. I hailed him, and asked the news from the fight; he replied by calling me by name, and I soon found it to be one of our citizens, well known to me, an officer in the Confederate army, but just before the breaking out of the war a strong Union man; he was elected as Union candidate to the State Convention from our county by an overwhelming vote, and I must do him the justice to say that at its first meeting he battled boldly against the Ordinance of Secession, and on many occasions, when it was not only unpopular, but dangerous to do so, he advocated the Union side. He yielded at last, and, like many other Union men, was forced by public sentiment into the army. "How is the contest going?" said I. He replied: "We have them all surrounded; but just before I left a movement was made by our troops to let them get away if they wished to do so. Orders were given to our regiment for every man to take care of himself. Our friend Wilson's son, a lad of fourteen, had his leg shot off, and I thought I would come and let the father know the condition of the son. A terrible time it was, I tell you; their men were vastly better drilled than ours; even when under fire they moved with as much precision as on the parade-ground, but ours broke ranks often. Moreover, you know I was a member of the Convention, and it would not do for me to be taken, and so I am here." A few officers came in during the night, and a Confederate surgeon, whom I well knew, when I met him the next morning, said that they were badly beaten; "the very earth trembled," said he, "when their infantry opened fire upon us." About 10 o'clock on Sunday morning the army, which a few days before had passed my house so exultant and confident of an easy and complete victory, came back; but it was an army no longer.

When Price went by at a quick march on his way to Boston Mountain, he was only falling back to lay a trap for his enemies; but now the army was a confused mob, not a regiment, not a company in rank, save two regiments of cavalry, which, as a rear guard, passed through near sundown; the rest were a rabble-rout, not four or five abreast, but the whole road about fifty feet wide perfectly filled with men, every one seemingly animated by the same desire to get away. Few, very few, had guns, knapsacks, or blankets; every thing calculated to impede their flight had been abandoned; many were hatless, and the few who had any thing to carry were those who had been fortunate enough to pick up a chicken, goose, or pig; if the latter, it was hastily divided so as not to be burdensome, and the usual formalities of butchering and taking off the bristles were dispensed with. Very few words were spoken; few of them had taken any food for two or three days; they had lost M'Culloch, M'Intosh, Slack, Reeves, and other officers of note, and, in a word, they were thoroughly dispirited. And thus, for hours, the human tide swept by a broken, drifting, disorganized mass, not an officer, that I could see, to give an order; and had there been, he could not have reduced that formless mass to discipline or order.

Many called in with piteous stories of suffering from hunger, and were relieved as far as our means would permit; but these soon failed, and all we could furnish was pure water. Four members of the 3d Louisiana stopped at one time to get water and one of them, looking round, said: "This is the largest number of our regiment that I have seen since we left the battle-field." Of another I inquired: "What has become of the 3d Louisiana?" he replied: "There is no 3d Louisiana." An old friend of mine— John Mays, a true Union man, whose pious care for some victims of a foul midnight murder, which will be noticed in the course of this narrative—who had three sons in the Confederate army, as I am fully assured, contrary to their wishes and principles, when he heard the sounds of battle, started for the field to see what was the fate of his boys, and was returning with one of them when I asked him, "How went the day?" replied he: "It was a perfect stampede; whole regiments threw down their arms and fled." Indeed, after the fall of M'Culloch and M'Intosh, and the capture of Col. Hebert, there was no one to take command of that portion of the army; the necessary result was the hurried and disorderly flight I have attempted to describe. The victors had no cavalry to keep up the pursuit, and, indeed, constant watching and fighting for three days had left them in such a condition that they were unable to reap all the advantages of their valor. Still it was a most decisive victory; much of that routed army never was got together again, and no portion of it made a stand, and then only to be again sorely beaten, till it had traversed the State from north to south, and crossed the Mississippi; escaping Curtis only to fall into the hands of Rosecrans and Grant. For several days after the battle squads of stragglers were going by, hundreds were scattered through the woods, and large numbers, instead of reporting to their respective regiments, returned to their homes. The houses in the line of the retreating army were filled with sick and wounded, the dead were left for the enemy to care for, and as the woods had taken fire during the action, numbers of the dead and such of the wounded as were not able to walk were burned.

In a few days scouting parties from the battle-field came to our town; several of the soldiers came to my house; some of them had been down with Gen. Asboth, and knew me, and of course were friendly. One of them claimed to have killed Ben M'Culloch, being familiar with the appearance of the rebel chief. I was curious to know whether he, who had sent the bitterest foe to Union men to his account, was really before me. I asked him to describe the person he had killed, and he described M'Culloch with as much precision as I could have done myself; every peculiarity of his dress, his white hat, black velvet, or velveteen suit, with long stockings drawn over boots and pantaloons up to his knees, were all mentioned; and as there was probably not another man in either army dressed like the Texan chief, I felt no doubt that his statement was correct. He said M'Culloch was sitting on his horse, with his glass to his eye, when he discovered him; he took deliberate aim, fired, and he fell. Southern men, who were near him when he was killed, state that he was observing the movements of the enemy through his field-glass when he received the fatal shot; thus corroborating the story of the Federal sharp-shooter. I did not ask him his name, but saw afterward in the report of the battle that it was Peter Pelican.

It is worthy of remark that the death of M'Culloch caused but little regret; he was extremely unpopular through all that region where he had so long held the chief command; his appearance was neither that of a great man nor a good soldier; his manners were coarse; his conversation thickly interlarded with oaths. I heard not a single strong expression of grief at his loss, but heard some of his own officers cursing his memory. At Wilson's Creek he suffered himself to be completely surprised by a foe not more than one-third his own number, and very narrowly escaped utter defeat. On his march back from Missouri to Arkansas he destroyed much valuable property in territory claimed by the Confederacy, and the north-west portion of Missouri and north-eastern Arkansas will long bear marks of his savage vandalism His own friends condemned his acts as cruel and unnecessary, for he really acted as if he had determined to yield the country he had been appointed to defend, and proving himself incapable to defend, he determined to destroy. And though, when the war shall close, we may see much to admire in the brave, but misguided M'Intosh, and not deny soldierly qualities to Slack, Reeves, and a host of others, who, though rebels, were not ruffians, it will be hard to find a single noble or redeeming quality to grace the name of Ben M'Culloch.

CHAPTER VII.

SECESSION PREACHERS.

Todd—Mitchell—Caples—Speech by a layman—A war-like chaplain.

FOR some weeks prior to the battle of Pea Ridge, great efforts were made to arouse the people of Arkansas to the necessity of speedily and largely reënforcing the army of Gen. Price, then in South-West Missouri. The agents for this purpose were mainly preachers—of these I heard the speeches of three; namely, Todd, Mitchell, and Caples, the first of these a man of but little speaking ability, and only a preacher on special occasions; but he was on the subject of secession a thorough fanatic—full of denunciations against the old flag, which he vilified and railed against with maniacal frenzy, full of apostrophes to the new flag; could prove secession from the Bible on almost every page; made special appeals to the ladies, had dreams and marvels in abundance to tell concerning the downfall of the old Government, and the speedy and glorious triumphs of the new. Any one to have believed him, must have supposed him to have the gift of prophecy; but with all his wonderful dreams and bright predictions he was not able to fire any great number with his own frenzy, and I do not think that Gen. Price's army was greatly increased through his endeavors. The second, Mitchell, from the neighborhood of Lexington, Mo., was really an engaging and effective speaker. I believe he had some position on Gen. Price's staff, and wore a feather in his hat, indicating that he fought with carnal weapons as well as those peculiar to the soldiers of the Prince of Peace. His appeals were truly eloquent and stirring; but our county had been to the last the stronghold of Unionism in the State, so much so, indeed, that recruits for the Union army were obtained in great numbers as soon as the boys in blue came among us; hence his success was not commensurate with his exertions. One peculiarity of his addresses was, that they were of the most bloodthirsty and personally-vindictive character; every man in the Federal ranks was little better than a demon, and he advocated not merely driving them back or taking them prisoners, but their utter destruction—not victory, but annihilation. He was a man, too, of good personal presence, had quite a dashing air, looked far more like a General than some who have passed my door; but truth must be told—some of his compatriots and fellow-soldiers did say that they always knew there was danger near at hand when they saw Mitchell's carriage ready and the horses' heads turned southward; in fact, that his movements were the harbingers of a retreat, and he was always in the advance of such a movement. Rev. Dr. Caples was also a man of marked ability, his purpose, like that of the others, to arouse Arkansians to the danger which threatened Price, and which must inevitably befall them in turn, unless they rallied to his aid and drove back the invaders, despoiled them of their arms and all the material of war; not a gun must be left in their hands, not an armed Dutchman left to pollute the soil; for the invaders, hundreds of them speaking with as little foreign accent as himself, and born, too, on this side of the water, were all Hessians; and the gravest charge against Lincoln was, that he was sending, not Americans, but the Dutch, to slaughter the free and noble sons of the South. The accent of these Teutonic mercenaries was ludicrously mimicked, their propensity to plunder and pillage descanted upon, enormities of the most aggravated character were charged upon them, and the prediction made that similar scenes would soon be enacted by them here unless the people should rise in their might and march to victory under the banner of the heroic Price, and yet the men did not volunteer; after one of his very able speeches, more highly colored, it is true, than facts warranted, yet well calculated to effect his purpose, I heard only one man offer to go, and he was drunk.

The reader will be curious to know how so much apathy with regard to going into the army can be made to agree with the fact that so many did enter. It was not the result of the inflammatory appeals of such men as these, but in consequence of a conscription law which few who came under its provisions could escape; a law which placed men in the ranks at the point of the bayonet, forcing in some cases those who, in consequence of ill health, were unable to endure the march to the camp. Some of these I knew before thus forced into a position most galling to them; some of the same I saw who took the very first opportunity to desert; and not a few of them afterward in the Federal service, which they entered from their own free choice, and the sincerity of which they subsequently proved in the face of the foe.

Another speech, though not by a preacher, made about this time, is worthy of a passing notice. One of our citizens—a man of huge proportions, and a far better talker than thinker, who at the beginning of the troubles was professedly a warm Union man, but who changed sides so frequently as to leave many in doubt as to his real sentiments—on one occasion, while the Southern feeling was in the ascendant, mounted a good's box in the public square, and having a powerful voice soon attracted a crowd. He urged upon them the importance of immediate organization, and seemingly convinced many of its necessity: one of the crowd cried out, "That's right, I am ready, and am going right by your side!" Now, going within range of a hostile gun had not entered into the orator's intention; he was for a moment disconcerted, but he rallied by explaining that though he was not going to the field himself, yet he was determined to defend the town to the last dire extremity. This opportunity was given on several occasions not long after, but he invariably got out of town just about the time the enemy got in. Having made known his unalterable determination to defend his home to his latest breath, he called upon the crowd to contribute to the equipment of those who expressed a readiness to go against the enemy. Up to the breaking out of the war, gold and silver had been almost our only currency, and the precious metals were still known; Confederate notes had been introduced among us, and by leading secessionists estimated at a little higher than the specie standard, as they were bearing eight per cent. interest. The people in the country, however, were very suspicious of the new money, and though some of them would receive it rather than be suspected as foes to the South, they suffered no opportunity of getting it into some more desirable form to pass unimproved. Now, it happened that the orator had a considerable amount of gold and silver in his pocket, some of which he exhibited in making his own contribution for arming and equipping the new volunteers; few seemed to be liberally disposed, till a farmer stepped up, and offering a Confederate five dollar bill said, "Well, I will give you two and a half;" the speaker took out a quarter eagle and gave to him in change, thanking him for his donation, and urging his example for the imitation of others. It was imitated speedily; the spirit of benevolence seemed to be suddenly awakened; but I observed that nearly every contribution was such as to make change in silver or gold necessary, while the benevolent tender was always in the shape of Confederate money. The fact was, the change received was far more desirable than the bill given; but the orator was so elated with his success that he did not see the point till he got out of change, and at that moment the liberality of his audience ceased as suddenly as it had begun. Poor, vain boaster! what terrible deeds he was wont to threaten, what an unconquerable spirit was his, if he were to be believed; and yet, when at last unable to escape when the enemy suddenly appeared, how meek he became, how ready to boast of his former Unionism!

From the preceding pages the reader will have learned that preachers, who entered into the work of rebellion, instead of attempting to mitigate in any degree the horrors of war, and to soothe the fierce passions which had been aroused, rather strove to increase the one and inflame still further the other. Preëminent among the ministers of the Gospel, who acted this unworthy part, was Dr. B. F. Hall, formerly of Kentucky, and well known throughout the West; of late years, however, a resident of Texas. When the Rangers came to join M'Culloch, prior to the battle of Pea Ridge, one regiment was commanded by a son of the venerable and sainted Barton W. Stone, whose apostolic purity of life and teaching are held in grateful remembrance by thousands. This son wore and disgraced the name of his father; and of his regiment, Elder B. F. Hall was chaplain. He had other aims, however, than to minister to the spiritual needs of the rude troopers; he rode a fine mule, carried a splendid rifle, and stipulated expressly that when there was any chance for killing Yankees he must be allowed the privilege of bagging as many as possible. I had known him in former years, and was not at all prepared for the change, which a few hours' intercourse was sufficient to convince me had taken place. In company with Elder Graham, I went down to meet him, at the house of a friend, on the evening of his arrival, and never was I so much amazed and shocked at what I heard and saw. A number of ladies were present in honor of the once famous preacher, but, alas, how fallen! He boasted of his trusty rifle, of the accuracy of his aim, and doubted not that the weapon, with which he claimed to have killed deer at two hundred yards, would be quite as effectual when a Yankee was the mark. Turning for a moment from this theme, he would compliment the ladies for their zeal and devotion to the cause of the South, as displayed in making clothing for the soldiers, in terms bordering on blasphemy; on one occasion comparing their labors with those who ministered to Christ in the days of his flesh. I ventured to ask what were his views concerning his brethren with and for whom he had labored in other years in the North and West. He replied they were no brethren of his, that the religionists on the other side of the line were all infidel, and that true religion was now only to be found in the South. Indeed, so extravagant were his denunciations of the people of the North that, had there been less method in his demonism, I should have charitably deemed him a monomaniac. Once during the evening he wished that the people of the North were upon one vast platform, with a magazine of powder beneath, and that he might have the pleasure of applying the match to hurl them all into eternity. Elder Graham was a man of fine social qualities, gifted in conversation and repartee; but that evening he was speechless, or nearly so, from the violence of the contending feelings of horror and disgust. To argue was not only useless, but dangerous, and we prudently, as we thought, said but little in reply; indeed, we thought it by no means safe to have our sentiments known by our quondam brother.

At another time he entertained the company with what I supposed at the outset was to be a tale illustrative of Southern nobility of character: he said that after the fight at Wilson's Creek, some of his Texas friends went over the battle-field, and falling in with a wounded Federal soldier, one of the party questioned him as to whether he would fight again if he recovered. The man, true to his country and flag, replied that he would; but instead, as I supposed the story would close by a tribute to a wounded but gallant foe, he said his friend Alf Johnson drew his revolver, and deliberately put a ball through the head of the helpless and wounded man. This he told with approval and with a chuckle and leer that a demon might have envied. He also urged that Kansas should be invaded and desolated. "What!" said I, "are you in favor of slaying unarmed and unresisting men?" "Yes," said he, "we will spare all the women and children, but give a grave to every man we find; if they are not armed when we find them they soon would be; they all must die." Yet no woman's voice was raised against this fiendish plan; and in the mind of my friend Graham there was a fierce struggle to repress the indignant expression of his feelings; and yet we should have been as mad as he who uttered such abominations, and far less prudent, had we given expression to our feelings, for he was among friends, but around us were foes. He then began to expatiate on the vandalism and cruelty of the Federal troops in Missouri, and told a most touching story to illustrate it. "A young man in the northern portion of that State was known to be well disposed to the Southern cause; one morning several of Lincoln's base hirelings stopped at the gate of his mother's house, for he was the only son of his mother, and she was a widow; they called for the son; he opened the door, and stood before them. 'Are you a Southern man?' was the rude demand. 'I am,' was the firm and noble reply. 'Will you dare to repeat that again?' said they. 'I dare,' was his reply. They raised their guns, and shot him where he stood. His old, heart-broken mother fell, in an agony of tears, upon the bleeding body of her slain boy, and, while uttering cries of anguish that would have melted hearts of stone, they brutally kicked her from the bleeding clay, with such violence as to break some of her ribs. And such creatures as these were to be sent to subdue the South, and enact there similar scenes of violence!"

The story was told most pathetically; tears glistened in the eyes of the ladies; a strong impression had been made; but my hour had come, and I seized it. Our host, who was sitting by me—one of the principal men of our town, a Kentuckian, and a great admirer of the late speaker—but a few days before had told me precisely the same story, all true, too, only it had occurred at Mount Vernon, about one hundred miles north of us, several hundred miles from the place where it had been located by the Rev. Hall. Moreover, I had heard the self-same story from another source; the fact was, it was a good stock story for the Southern cause; but in the last instance it had been located with the utmost precision at an entirely different point from that designated by both the others. I had, therefore, a fine opportunity, as the friend of truth, to step in and dry the tears which were starting by discrediting the whole matter, which I did as follows: "The story you have related," said I, "is a very touching one, and withal very circumstantial; but I was told the same story, with all the particulars which attaches to yours, a few days since, with this single difference, that it occurred just up here at Mount Vernon." I was ready to lay my hand on our host's shoulder as my authority, had there been any dispute, and left them to settle the little discrepancy of several hundred miles as best they could. No one spoke, however, and I proceeded: "I heard the same story from another quarter, but it was located at an entirely different point from that in the other two accounts, and I am beginning to think it likely that an event, which took place in so many different localities, never occurred at all." There was a dead silence; the emotion had all vanished; every one felt how awkward it would be to explain the matter, the subject was dropped, conversation on other themes was attempted, but soon flagged; cold water had been thrown upon the whole affair, and the company soon dispersed.

When Graham and myself got out of doors, he asked me how I felt; my reply was: "As if I had been in the company of a highwayman." He had never met Dr. Hall before, but had heard much of him, and had fully expected to meet a polished Christian gentleman; he had met with a rude ruffian, and had been obliged to choke down the indignant expression of outraged feeling till the tears were ready to flow.

On another occasion, shortly before the Pea Ridge battle, he declared that the men of Texas ought to go up against those invaders, and not only slay them, but cut off their right hands and bring them home tied to their saddle skirts. He went up to the Pea Ridge fight, but I think took no very active part, save such as was necessary to get away. I saw him on the day that the shattered and broken fragments of M'Culloch's army passed southward, never to return; but O how changed, how crestfallen! he had predicted a splendid triumph, and their discomfiture had been utter and complete. The tones of his

voice were soft and subdued, his face looked care-worn and hag-
gard, his beard more grizzly, his hat more slouched; and the last
time I remember seeing him he was engaged in mildly chiding
one of the Confederate captains, who was cursing M'Culloch,
who had been killed a few days before, charging all their disas-
ters upon him. I don't think he succeeded in calming the captain; he seemed to grow more furious under the reproof, and
the last words I heard him utter was the benevolent hope that
Ben M'Culloch was in hell.

CHAPTER VIII.

GUERRILLAS.

Roving bands—The midnight murder—Smith and his negroes—Assassination of Neal—Retaliation.

IT was not till after the battle of Pea Ridge and the departure of the Union army southward that we were troubled by guerrillas; but soon after that event they began their deeds of violence and blood. Many of them were men who had left Missouri with Price, and, after he had been driven thence, were unwilling to cross the Mississippi with him and follow his waning fortunes; nor could they with safety return to their own State. Others, under different partisan chiefs, attached to no army, had been driven from South-West Missouri, and, being destitute of the organization and supplies of an army, they degenerated into predatory bands, roving hither and thither on much the same principle that regulates the movements of the wandering Arabs. Some of these bands were well mounted, simply because every man took a horse when he fancied him, little caring whether it belonged to friend or foe; if a friend, he could certainly spare a horse for a cause in which he was willing to risk life and undergo every privation; if a foe, the animal was lawful spoil. Not being incumbered with supply trains, they could move with celerity, but wherever they encamped they left unmistakable evidences of their presence; no commissary or quarter-master doled out to them a small ration for man or beast; if what they needed was in reach it was used without stint, each being judge of his own necessities. At one time several of these bands met together and encamped in our town. They numbered not far from one thousand, being composed of the commands of Rains, Coffee, Hughes, Cockerell, and others. There was but little of the strictness of military discipline observed among them; even their leaders were far from being united in their objects and purposes, and the only unanimity they exhibited was a desire to move in the same direction when they heard that a body of Federal cavalry was on their track; their movements then were generally swift and secret, and for the most part in an opposite direction. Once a portion of them made a raid into Missouri, and gained quite a victory at Lone Jack; but being pursued they were obliged to leave much of their plunder behind; and some of them declared, when they returned, that they had not unsaddled their horses for a week. They were so pressed that they were unable to care for their wounded, and many were overtaken and captured, some of them asleep on their horses. The leaders of those bands, though in some instances men of ability, were mostly intemperate, and when under the influence of drink perpetrated crimes, which we fain would hope they would have shrunk from in their sober moments. On one occasion, about the last of June, the bands of Coffee, Rains, and some others came into our town, bringing as prisoners several men whom they had taken from their homes while endeavoring to secure their crops; the men were accused of no crime, and were engaged in their usual peaceful labors when arrested. A few days after they were brought in, Coffee, who was seldom sober, and some of the other officers, began to talk about shooting those prisoners in retaliation for some men they had lost in an engagement with some Federal cavalry a few days before. They mutually excited each other while in their cups, and even in the hearing of some citizens spoke of shooting their prisoners; their friends regarded their threats as due more to the liquor they had taken than any serious intention to injure innocent men; but no, the drunken wretches were in earnest, and before

the dawn of another morning they had executed their murder-
ous purpose.

About midnight, without the least form of trial or intimation of the fate that awaited them, the prisoners, four in number, were marched southward under a strong guard; about a mile
from town they turned into a dim and unfrequented road, and
when about a quarter of a mile from the main road were halted.
On the lower side of the road was a comparatively clear spot,
the undergrowth having been cleared away; into that space they
were ordered, the word was given, the report of fifteen or twenty
guns was heard, they all fell, and their murderers returned and
left them just as they lay. The firing was heard in town, but the
cause of it was known only to the drunken and brutal Coffee
and his companions, by whose order this deed, black as the hour
at which it took place, was done.

Only three of the poor wretches, however, were dead, the
other was shot through the body and fell; and after the departure of the executioners he crawled through the bushes and over
the rocks about a quarter of a mile to the nearest house; his
wounds were of a horrible character, and no expectation was
entertained that he could live more than a few hours. In this
condition, with death, as he felt assured, close at hand, he told
his sad story; he said that he and his companions had never had
arms in their hands on either side, that they were taken prisoners at home while at work, that they knew of no reason for their
arrest, but, without warning and without crime, had been torn
from their families; they had not been tried, and only knew their
fate when brought to the place of the foul murder. He gave his
name and that of his fellow-prisoners, and desired that their
families might be informed of their fate. A few hours more would
in all probability have brought an end to his sufferings; but the
next day the news got out that one of the victims was still alive;
some of the band rode out to see him, and one of them gave him
some drug which soon resulted in a sleep from which he never

awoke again; the shooting at midnight was doubtless consummated by deliberate poisoning in open day.

The bodies of the other three were found weltering in their blood by some of the neighbors the next morning, whose fears and suspicions had been aroused by the firing in such an unfrequented place at an hour so unusual, who immediately set about to give them a burial, hasty it is true, but decent as circumstances would permit.

They were proceeding in their pious task, preparing a grave large and deep enough for the three; but before the task was half accomplished, the murderers of the previous night came upon them, made them throw the bodies into the half-dug grave, and would not permit them to hide with earth the bodies of the poor victims from the light of day and the reach of dogs and vultures. One of the burial party, however, an old man, and a Union man, after their departure, came back and built a wall of loose stones around the place of the dead, and so protected it with brush that the bodies could not be disturbed by brute or obscene birds.

Noble old man! hard didst thou toil in thy abor of love in the heat of that Summer day; no human eye saw thy sweat and toil, or knew the thoughts of thy heart as thou didst labor at the grave of the murdered ones; but the honest and noble purpose of thy heart, and the pious labor of thy hands, were not unnoted of God; and that little mound thou didst raise over those strangers with sad heart in that solitude will seem, to thy fellows even, a mountain peak raising thee nearer to heaven than thou ever didst stand before.

After a few visits from bands like these the secessionists learned that in every thing, except the name, they were as much to be feared as the Federals themselves; they took what they wanted, or could find; stopped as long as they pleased, and departed without any settlement; in fact, they had no military chest, and payment to either friend or foe was entirely out of the question. Their roving, predatory life had a most fearful effect on their morals; an army has never been regarded as a school of virtue; but these exceeded all others that I have ever met with. I have frequently seen large bodies of men in camp, and profanity may be almost called the language of the camp, but I feel confident that I have seen more card-playing and heard more blasphemy in one day among a few hundred men of Rains's and Coffee's command, than in ten times the number of other commands, in ten times that period.

Some of the men composing these bands I was shocked to learn belonged to families of the highest respectability, but now so filthy, squalid, and profane that the friends of other days would have found it most difficult to recognize them. Nor were these traits redeemed by the single virtue of courage or even recklessness, for ever and anon a heavy scout of hostile cavalry would sweep down upon them, and it was no uncommon thing to hear them boast of the celerity of their flight; and though in many instances they largely outnumbered their foes, I do not recollect a single instance in which they had reason to plume themselves upon their bravery. One lovely night in Summer, I well remember, the moon was nearly full; in the Confederate camp at bedtime there was not the remotest idea of leaving us for some time; indeed, they were far better pleased with our town than the citizens were with them. Many rose the next morning, doubtless expecting to see them there still, but they were miles away and no enemy near; indeed, they managed not to let them get dangerously near. In this instance they numbered about thirteen hundred, while the enemy, who came some two days after, numbered but seven hundred.

The truth is they were sick of the war; they had ample opportunities of entering the Confederate service, and were even appealed to upon that subject; but no, when they took up arms they never expected to leave Missouri, there was nothing alluring in the swamps of Mississippi; their great thought was to get back home, and in the expectation of being able to do so they lingered upon the border. In this, however, they were doomed to disappointment, for others were driven out, and

many left with their movable property, showing quite a dispo-
sition to abandon Missouri as hopeless, rather than a desire to
win her for the brightest star in the Confederate galaxy. The
tier of border counties was almost depopulated, and it was sad,
most sad, to see families who, one year and a half before,
expected to lay their bones in the family graveyard, abandoning homes once most delightful, and seeking others in the far,
far West. Most of the fugitives had their slaves with them as
companions of their flight, and these latter, indeed, were in most
cases the cause of it. And yet, though slaves had become a very
uncertain kind of property, men would abandon home, kindred,
friends, every thing, in fact, to save their negroes. As there were
but few slaves in our county—which may be one of the reasons
why it was the strongest Union county in the State—but few
of our citizens joined the tide of emigrants going southward;
occasionally, however, one would go.

One of these, whom we shall call Smith, had but one negro,
and he so dwarfed in the lower extremities, that, though he
looked like a man when sitting, he had only the stature of a child
when on his feet. To all new-comers this negro was a curiosity;
without bending his knees he could so bend his body as to pick
up a small coin from the ground with his lips, and many a dime
did he make by his skill in this particular. It is said that Smith,
accompanied by the aforesaid negro, was met by a neighbor but
a short distance from town, evidently on his way to Texas, and
on being asked where he was going, replied, that "he was taking
his negroes South." Certain it is that Smith and the black dwarf
were seen among us no more. His wife and children followed
sometime after, but I never heard whether they succeeded in
overtaking the husband and "his negroes."

Another had a very intelligent yellow man, named John,
among his numerous slaves; he became convinced of the necessity of going further south in order to retain them, and sent John
to get the mules and team for the journey. John started, but did
not get back in time to accompany his master, who, hearing that

the Federals were approaching, set out in great haste, leaving the servant-man behind. John disappeared; many spoke of his ingratitude in deserting his master in the hour of need; but after a few days the Federal troops came in and John made his appearance, procured a wagon, put his baggage and his wife into it, and drove away, a happy fellow, when the army returned North again. There were a few others whose blacks were liberated by the coming of the Union army, who felt that they themselves were greatly gainers by the change; the problem of emancipation had been one most difficult of solution, and when that solution came, in a manner so unexpected, it was most welcome.

Another murder, darker, and more unprovoked, if possible, than the foul midnight deed narrated a few pages back, took place a few miles from town; and as the subject of it was well known for miles around, it struck a strange and undefinable terror into nearly every household; for if such persons, as the victim in this instance, were not safe, there were none who could feel secure.

He was an aged man by the name of Neal, a leading member of the Methodist Church, of simple manners and a pure life, well and widely known, and universally regarded as a good man. He was a Union man, as nearly all of his type of character were, and yet he was not offensively so; he did not boast of his attachment to the old Government, nor did he speak harshly or bitterly of his neighbors who favored the rebellion. He was too old and of too pacific a spirit to take up arms, and ready at all times to relieve the wants of the sick and suffering without reference to their position on the great questions of the day.

No intemperate language, no unfriendly act was charged upon him; his only crime, he had never wavered in his attachment to the Government, he never had approved of the mad act of secession, but yielding to the violence of a storm that he was powerless to resist, he retained his principles in a day of very general defection, and for this, at last, he became one of the noble army of martyrs for the Union, whose graves are to be found all over the seceded States, whom generations to come will yet honor.

One afternoon several mounted men, friendly to all appearance, rode up to his gate, asking food for themselves and animals; they were invited to alight and remain till provision could be made for their wants; they entered the house, and found some two or three men there, relatives of the family, and entered freely into conversation with them, but not giving the slightest intimation as to which party they were attached. Supper was served; they all sat down and partook; at its close, the strangers said that Gen. Curtis, whose army was encamped some twenty or thirty miles northward, had heard that he, Neal, had been giving information to the Southern army, and that he must go with them to the Federal camp to answer to this charge. The old man, with all the fearlessness of innocence, expressed his willingness to go, but his wife was fearful, she scarce knew why; the strangers, however, insisted that he and the men who were at the house should go with them instantly to the camp, tied their hands behind them, and they, riding, with the captives on foot before them, set off.

They had only proceeded a few hundred yards, when they halted their prisoners, formed them in a line, and informed them that if they had any prayers to offer they had better begin, as they had only five minutes to live. Appalled by this intelligence, they began to plead for their lives; the old man prayed them to spare him, but they were deaf to his entreaties; suddenly one of the younger prisoners, seeing death inevitable, by a violent effort broke the ropes which confined his hands, and ran for the woods and escaped; upon this the murderers fired upon the rest, killing the old man and wounding the others, and then hastily abandoned the scene of blood. They were Confederates, and had endeavored to palm themselves off as Union soldiers, had been hospitably entertained, and rode off with the blood of their innocent and unsuspecting host upon their hands.

This was the first killing of a private and unarmed citizen

that had taken place, and the sensation it produced was immense; as soon as it was known, those who gathered around the evening fire in nearly every house and cabin looked anxiously into each other's faces, and spoke in low tones of the dead, and their own probable future. If a stranger or two rode up to a dwelling, wives and mothers became fearful, and children turned ghastly pale; none knew who would be the next victim, and a shadow seemed to have fallen upon every household.

Soon other murders, almost as wanton, were heard of, and then the inevitable result, fierce and swift retaliation. Union men who had been driven from their homes, and hunted like wild beasts, and even some who had been deemed dead, suddenly made their appearance among us, dressed in the National uniform, leading Federal scouting parties, and bitter was the vengeance they inflicted upon the authors of their wrongs. Fully acquainted with the country, they pursued their former persecutors to their most secret haunts, and in many instances meted out to them the fate they had so narrowly escaped. Had a Union man been killed, the slayer, if known, was a doomed man; had the family of a Union man been disturbed, or his house pillaged, woe to the perpetrators, if they were known, when those bold riders came back to the homes which the conscript law had compelled them for a season to desert.

I am no apologist for the fierce and unsparing law so fearfully and rigidly enforced as it was in many instances; I merely give the facts, in order that the reader may have some idea of the state of things peculiar, not only to our region, but experienced in portions of the whole South. Some of the scouting parties, I am well assured, on both sides, did not incumber themselves with prisoners. The bands of Coffee, Jackman, and other Missourian partisan chiefs had become so obnoxious on account of their depredations upon life and property, that they were shot down wherever they were found.

One morning while visiting at a farm not far from town, I was greatly surprised to see a man in the usual Confederate garb approaching the house, unarmed, and with a strange, unsteady gait; when he came nearer he was recognized as a Missouri soldier, who but a few days before had sought and found refuge there from Union troops then in the vicinity. He was tired of the war, and desirous of getting home to his family; he, with a friend who sought refuge at the same time and place, as soon as they heard of the withdrawal of the Union troops, determined to make their way home if possible; he came back alone as described, and when he got nearer we discovered that he had been wounded, and on examination we found a bullet-hole in the back part of the skull; and he gave the following account of himself and comrade. They had got several miles on their way, and had stopped at a house for the night; about midnight several men entered and took them both prisoners, and ordered them to walk before them to the camp; after proceeding some distance the prisoners were directed to turn into a by-path; this they pursued for some time—the heads of their captors' horses almost touching them—when, without a word of warning, they were fired upon, and fell. The horsemen rode on, not dismounting to see whether life was extinct; and the survivor states that he stretched out his hand and reached his companion, found him still breathing, but unable to speak; soon he ceased to breathe, and the wounded man arose and wandered about till he came to a house, where his wound was dressed; but its occupants thought it dangerous for both should he remain, and he reached the place where I met him in the condition I have stated, leaving his companion unburied where he fell. From the nature of his wound I thought it impossible for him to survive; but procuring the services of a surgeon, he so far recovered in a few weeks as to start for Missouri again; whether he was more successful in this attempt than in the first I have never learned. Such is one of the ten thousand sad histories enacted on the border, and hundreds of those who left Missouri in arms will never be heard of again till all the graves shall give up their dead.

CHAPTER IX.

REBELS—RUMORS—RAIDS.

Secession orators—Marvelous stories—Escape of Tebbetts and Graham—Weary days—Sick soldiers.

IT may have occurred to the reader, that I have not acted justly in failing to chronicle the achievements of the men in our region most prominent in the cause of the South. True, they have occupied but little space on these pages, but they shall remain in obscurity no longer. Yet truth compels me to state that those who raised their voices first and loudest for the secession of the State, and in favor of a Southern Confederacy, were not as lavish of their blood as of their words. By their specious arguments they induced others to peril their lives for what they taught them were their rights, but in very few instances did they prove themselves possessed of that courage they were so ready to applaud in others.

Two prominent members of the legal profession, A. M. Wilson and W. D. Reagan, were among the first and boldest speakers on the disunion side. The unwarlike spirit of the people of the North, the boundless resources of the South, the assurance that secession would be peaceable, and the certainty of foreign interference if war should come, pictures of the extension of slavery, the acquisition of Mexico, and the unexampled prosperity of the South, under the new order of things, were the arguments relied upon to decide the wavering and confirm those already committed to Southern views. But of their wealth, of which they had abundance, they gave little to the cause which they advocated with such noisy zeal; and of their precious blood they were even still more careful. They were near the battle-field of Wilson's Creek when the fight began, but when it closed they were miles away. When Price and his retreating legions passed southward in full retreat, they were in that army, if not of it. One of them, W. D. Reagan, was the author of the false charges which caused the arrest of Judge Tebbetts, previously narrated; charges which he did not even attempt to prove on the trial, and the change of public sentiment with regard to the accused, doubtless, was owing in a great measure to the fact that he overshot the mark by relying upon unfounded rumors, and consulting his own feelings and desires rather than the truth in the charges which he made.

This same gentleman on one occasion was haranguing a crowd composed certainly not of the most enlightened and influential of his fellow-citizens, and for that very reason they were best suited to his designs. In order to demonstrate that the South was not only able to maintain a separate existence, but to ruin the North, or to starve her into submission, if necessary, he thus made reference to the staples of the South: "Whar, my friends, do you get your cotton? Whar do you get your rice? Whar do you get your sugar?" One of his auditory, whose mind was concerned, doubtless, with regard to a more necessary and interesting staple, cried out, in a voice which sounded like the very echo of the speaker's, and which but gave utterance to the thoughts of many present, "And whar do you get your whisky?"

Nor was his unwillingness to shed his blood for the cause for which he so loudly contended unnoted. One of his fellow-citizens, who had observed this peculiarity, approached him one day and informed him that they were engaged in raising a company, and asked him if he would take the command of it. Stretching his tall figure to the utmost, by rising on his toes, he brought his heels down to the pavement with the emphatic and withering declaration, "Sir, I am not to be coerced into measures!" Notwithstanding that Federal scouts were scouring the country, and ever and anon dashing into town, and always at a moment when the citizens were least expecting them, those gentlemen always contrived to keep out of harm's way, till, tired of continued excitements and alarms, they abandoned the country they had done so much to ruin.

The most active men in the war were those who had been Union men, and had resisted the passage of the Ordinance of Secession. When they saw war and ruin impending they identified themselves with their State rather than with their country, feeling at the time, like Stephens of Georgia, that the action of the State was without just cause, and must result disastrously, and yet preferred going down with, to abandoning, the vessel. Some of these were men of wealth, position, and influence, whose Unionism no one doubted, and who only yielded when it would have been madness to resist; but how much better would it have been had they, like other and wiser men, left for regions where thought and speech were still free, before the storm in its fury burst upon them! I am aware how difficult it is to understand how these things could really be so; yet to me it is not stranger than to find men at the North who lift neither hand nor voice in favor of the Government which blesses and protects them; nay, more, who rail against its measures and sympathize with its foes. The former clung to their State, and periled all when the State was wrong; the latter oppose State and Nation, when both are right. The former are called rebels; it would be an abuse of language to call the latter loyal.

The tales which were circulated and believed will long remain as a monument of the infatuation and credulity of the people. Soon after the war broke out, all the ordinary avenues of information were closed; newspapers a month old were eagerly sought after, and these, too, mainly from Missouri; and I have known five dollars offered and refused for a single copy of the St. Louis Republican. Persons living within one hundred miles of each other were not able to communicate for months together, and as a necessary consequence rumor supplied the place of news.

As a specimen of what was gravely told, and by many believed, I will instance the following: The Potomac Army was utterly routed, eighty thousand prisoners taken, among them Gen. M'Clellan and staff. In one night thirteen iron gun-boats laden with rich cargoes ran into Mobile. Recognition by France and England took place every few weeks, and the last account was unquestionably true. Washington City was, time and again, in the hands of the Confederates. A French fleet was lying before New Orleans, and thirty days were given to the Federal Government in which to close the war; if this was not done hostilities were to begin immediately. Then news of great and terrible disaffection, amounting in many cases to absolute mutiny in the various armies of the North, came to our ears; the whole State of Illinois was in a state of revolt, the Great Central Railway torn up in many places to prevent the transportation of soldiers southward; nay, whole regiments stacked their arms, and refused to fight any longer for the subjugation of their Southern brethren; the names and numbers of these regiments were given with the utmost precision, and—will it be credited?—in some instances by Northern men, recent converts to secession doctrines, who really seemed to believe these monstrous fabrications to be true. And what seemed stranger still, instead of frequent disappointment producing skepticism, it only prepared them for swallowing stories still more improbable. Indeed, I have been amazed again and again, at that strange, and to me, even now, unaccountable perversity, which led men, in the soundness of whose judgment I once had the greatest confidence, to receive with the most unhesitating faith as matters of fact the wildest and most improbable of fictions, which seemed so to me the moment I heard them.

One of the most widely circulated and firmly believed of these rumors was the death of Gen. Sigel at the battle of Pea Ridge; the evidence upon this point was deemed incontrovertible—to doubt it was proof that the doubter was not a sound Southern man. The nature of his wound was described, the superb coffin in which the corpse was placed, and in which it was transmitted to St. Louis for burial, were dwelt upon with the greatest minuteness—not a link was wanting in the chain of evidence which was adduced to prove the death of the redoubtable German. Nay, on one occasion when I ventured the remark that there might be some doubt in the matter, as the papers contained accounts of his visit to Washington, and also a speech delivered by him in New York, I was met in solid earnest by the reply that those accounts had doubtless been prepared to conceal from the Northern public the loss of one of their ablest generals. In a word, the infatuation was complete; improbability was no longer the slightest barrier in the way of belief.

During the Summer of 1862 our region was the scene of frequent raids, by scouting parties from both armies. Many of the Missouri troops who had enlisted in the service of the State were unwilling to join the Confederate army, and they remained on the border awaiting a favorable opportunity to return. Many of the roving bands from that State being closely pursued by the Federal cavalry came into Arkansas, and united with those already there. The Federals held Cassville and Springfield, and sent frequent scouting parties down to observe the motions of the various guerrilla bands; and so frequent were the visits from both parties, that we often found it difficult to determine whether we were under Jeff. Davis or Lincoln rule. Sometimes we were under neither.

One day it was the Stripes and Stars; the next it might be, and often was, the stars and bars. Indeed, I well remember one occasion, when some of us were congratulating each other on the prospect of quiet for a few days or weeks, that, while yet speaking, our eyes were greeted and our ears saluted by the ring and flash of steel, and the town was in possession of an armed force. The frequency of these changes rendered the citizens of different views extremely tolerant of each other; neither party knew how long the other might be in the ascendency; and though the warmth of former friendship was neither felt nor expressed, the bitterness of past enmity was, if not forgotten, at least restrained. After some weeks of unusual quiet, when many Southern men had returned to their homes, which they had long regarded as insecure, Major Hubbard, of the Eighth Missouri Cavalry, dashed suddenly into the town before any one could escape; every outlet was carefully guarded, and quite a number who had been in the army, and some still in actual service, were captured; indeed, nearly every man in town was arrested, and required to give an account of himself. I was among that number; but it was not an irksome captivity, for as soon as my name was mentioned to Major Hubbard, I was released in a most courteous manner. Not so with a large number of others: they had been so committed to the rebellion that it was necessary to retain them as prisoners, and quite a number were informed that it would be necessary to go to Head-Quarters at Springfield. Some little surprise was expressed that Judge Tebbetts was not arrested; but Major Hubbard, before leaving, gave him a public arrest, which lasted, however, but for a few moments. Many Southern men, when arrested, sought the interposition of Judge Tebbetts, whose influence was very powerful in their behalf; in many instances that influence was exerted and their release procured; but jealous eyes were watching, and his kindness came near proving his overthrow. Although the good offices of Union men were sought and enjoyed, the very fact of their having influence enough to procure favors, which, in some cases, were not appreciated as they should have been, aroused the hitherto concealed hatred of men whose acts would have justly entitled them to a place among the prisoners sent under guard to Springfield.

Some of those men, the night after the departure of the Union troops, held a secret meeting, in which the death of Judge

Tebbetts, myself, and one or two others, by hanging, was proposed. This plot happily came to the knowledge of a lady friend
of Judge Tebbetts, who gave him warning. The character of those
who were engaged in it was such, that he had every reason to
believe that they would attempt its execution; no time remained
for consultation with his friends, and in a few moments after he
was on his way to the Federal lines, which he soon reached in
safety; but for months was cut off from all intercourse with his
family.

Not long after this Elder Graham, whose Union principles
were well known, feeling that his remaining was not safe, and
in the hope of finding a refuge for his family, which he could
not by any possibility then take with him, determined to try to
escape; the roads were all guarded, and the attempt was not
unattended with danger; but there was great danger in remaining, so he made the effort.

At the breaking out of the war he was in easy circumstances,
but affairs were now so changed that he was obliged to borrow
ten dollars to bear his expenses. He expected to find it difficult
to pass Bentonville, which was between him and the Federal
lines, and where he was well known; but instead of avoiding it,
he rode up amid a crowd of secessionists who were at the tavern, gave the landlord his saddle-bags, and told him to put up
his horse, and, in a tone that all could hear, asked concerning
a lady relative of his whose husband was in the Confederate
army, and started to pay her a short visit. Soon returning he
made some inquiries concerning a man who lived a few miles
from there, as if about to visit him, and asked what course to
take so as to avoid falling in with the Federal scouts. A Masonic
brother was of great service to him at that juncture, pledging
himself to check any pursuit of him if possible.

He started, but soon left the main road, and traveled where
the leaves were thickest, and sometimes riding quite a distance
in the bed of a narrow stream, so as to leave no trace of his
course. He passed the night at the house of an old friend, but

who was now a bitter secessionist, and of course did not reveal his purpose. The next day, avoiding all public roads, he reached Keetsville—a place noted for many a dark deed—and during the evening saw provisions carried, from the house in which he was stopping, to guerrillas who were concealed in the woods not far distant for the purpose of shooting any Federal who might come down the road, or any refugee going up in the direction of the Federal lines. His landlord who was evidently in communication with those outlaws, intimated to him that it was dangerous to travel in that direction; but to return now was as dangerous as to go forward, and the next morning, in a heavy storm, he set out for Cassville, then held by Federal troops. Two men had preceded him but a few hours, and one came riding back in great haste, saying, that they had been fired upon and his companion killed. My friend soon came to a little pool of blood which marked the spot where the foul deed was done, but the body and the murderers had disappeared. An hour or two earlier and he might have met the same fate. Every moment was now precious; he rode on at a rapid pace, soon met the Federal pickets, and was safe.

Before leaving he laid his purpose before me, and my wife urged me to go with him, as she was in continual fear for me, but I could not consent to leave a wife and two little children in a place so fraught with danger to myself, and therefore determined to wait in hope of an opportunity to leave together; but the opportunity seemed to be long delayed; the days and weeks seemed much longer after the escape of my friends, and I knew that my own movements were become the subject of closer scrutiny than ever before.

The days now became intolerably long; almost the only friends with whom I could speak freely were gone; we had been accustomed to meet almost daily to talk over the course which events seemed taking, and when we were so fortunate as to get a newspaper, its contents were eagerly devoured; frequently our readings took place with closed doors and blinds, and if the news was particularly cheering, an effort had to be made to seem less elated than we really were.

Elder Graham, prior to his leaving, had preached at least twice per month; and his preaching and prayers, once so popular and unquestioned, became the theme of the severest criticism. It had not escaped the observation of some of the warm advocates of secession, that his prayers were much the same as before the war broke out; the Confederacy, its army, and executive were never mentioned, and the reason of this was obvious to many. On one occasion, just after he had preached, he was interrogated in such a manner as to render a reply indispensable. "Mr. Graham," said a secessionist, "why do you not pray for our rulers and army?" He replied, "There is only one Scriptural ground on which I could do so." "What may that be?" "Why," said he, "we are instructed to pray for our enemies." The question was also proposed to myself, Why do you not pray for the success of our arms? because, was the reply, the Almighty does not seem to have declared in favor of them, and prayers to that effect would seem more like instructions than petitions.

Better answers by far than these can be well imagined by the reader; but under the circumstances they were the best that could be given. One minister in our town took the ground, that the whole proceedings in the case were wrong, that the Bible absolutely condemned war, and that Christians should take no part in it, and he himself was consistent enough to take no other part than the manufacture of cartridges for the rebel army, and this he did for months together.

A prominent member of one of the Churches was one day uttering some very bloodthirsty speeches, when he was asked by a bystander what became of the injunction to love our enemies? to which the reply was given, that a different kind of enemies must be meant than those we had to deal with.

As a refuge from the monotony which became most oppressive, as well as to keep out of discussions, which often betrayed me into expressions imprudent and dangerous, I had gathered some dozen or more children together and began teaching, but under circumstances very different from which I had pursued that occupation before. Our College, with its spacious hall and lecture-rooms, was exchanged for a building that had been hastily improvised as a kitchen by the Southern troops when quartered in our town; it was in the midst of the grove in which our beautiful buildings once stood, and often brought painfully to remembrance the different scenes I had witnessed upon the same ground, never however, to be repeated.

I, moreover, continued my labors as a minister, and, as service had long been suspended in all the other churches, my congregations were quite respectable in numbers, and comprised persons of quite different religious sentiments, and this I continued nearly as long as I remained. And from all I was able to learn, there was not another school or Church meeting in all that region.

Save that a scouting party, from one side or the other, dashed into, or swept through our town, the Summer passed quietly by; every day marked by a Sabbath-like stillness, and our late flourishing little city presenting almost the desolation of a desert. Nor can it be doubted that the scene, just hinted at in the above sketch, is but too faithful a picture of what was taking place in many other portions of the Confederacy. Schools and institutions of learning broken up, churches abandoned, the Sabbath unnoted, every thing around, indeed, denoting a rapid lapse into barbarism, all trade at an end, nearly all travel suspended, the comforts of life nearly all gone, the absolute necessaries difficult to be obtained, altogether made a picture difficult to be realized in a country which has not been made the scene of war. But when the end shall come the people of both sections will be able to realize far more vividly than now what a fearful scourge is war, and the lesson, I doubt not, will be so impressive as to create in the minds of all who have witnessed its desolating influence an earnest desire for lasting peace.

One sad token of the war, a scene of melancholy interest,

still remained; a number of sick and wounded men whom the Confederates were unable to remove were left in the Female Seminary, then used as a hospital. Their situation was most pitiable, they were destitute of nearly every thing their condition required; and though a surgeon was left with them, I never saw him by the bedside of his patients, although I visited them almost daily with whatever I could command that would minister to their comfort. Nor can I say that they received the attention they might have expected from our citizens whose battles they had been fighting; a few, and but a few, seemed to have any sympathy for them; and deserted by their companions in arms, little cared for by those for whom they had braved the diseases of the camp and the dangers of the field, without careful and cheerful nurses, far, far from home, and the prospect of return distant, they died rapidly, and there were no loved ones near to lament their fate. To me it is and ever will be a pleasant reflection that I did all in my power to aid and comfort them. I have seen eyes, over which the mists of death were fast stealing, brighten at my entrance, and thin, pale hands raised while voices faint and faltering blessed me. I have made the long, painful hours seem shorter to many, and smoothed in some cases the path to the grave. God knows they needed a hundred-fold more care than they received, but I feel that I withheld nothing that it was in my power to impart.

This experience of mine gave me an opportunity of noting the spirit of many of the Southern soldiers, and I must say that they bore themselves neither as heroes nor martyrs; there was an entire lack of enthusiasm for the cause in which they had battled, no hope as to the final result. Not one, that I now recollect, expressed a wish to rejoin his companions in arms in the field of danger; the only strong desire was a wish to get home. For this feeling several causes may be assigned; they did not, and could not, feel that they had ever been despoiled of a single right by the Government they were endeavoring to destroy; nor had they ever received any blessings from the one which, at the mandate of their despotic leaders, they were endeavoring to establish. They permitted themselves to be aroused by the recital of imaginary wrongs; they had trusted the promises of leaders which they soon perceived must remain unfulfilled. They saw how little their comfort was cared for in camp or hospital; poorly clad, poorly armed, poorly fed, poorly paid—for these were all true of the trans-Mississippi army—with the knowledge brought home, by experience on the part of many of them, that they had unwisely bartered true liberty for a tyrant's rule; their illusive dreams of the future all banished by stern and sad reality, they sighed only for peace and home.

CHAPTER X.

THE MARCH AND BATTLE.

The madman—The army and its doings—Herron's forced
march—Night before the battle—Battle of Prairie Grove.

AMONG those left behind by the retreating army was one
whose reason had fled. At times he was violent, and it was next
to impossible to keep him under restraint; manacles were broken, ropes and chains seemed powerless to bind him, and,
though a small man, his efforts to free himself from restraint
were astonishing. At one time he would be quite rational, and
his conversation indicated quite a cultivated mind; at other
times he was subject to fits of the wildest frenzy. There was
scarcely a house in the town that he did not visit, often effecting his entrance so quietly as to take the family by surprise.
Sometimes he would take possession of a vacant dwelling, give
a party in imagination, have the house illuminated, and sing,
and rave, and howl till perfectly exhausted. He was known
among us as "Wild Bill," and though a terror to many he never
sought to injure those who treated him kindly. He gave every
one a name according to his fancy, and we soon had many of
the great names of history among us, as well as a number of the
notable ones of the present; and it was too much for our gravity sometimes to see him in conversation, as he thought, with
men long since dead, or with famous generals or statesmen still
living; to Bill, however, it was all real, and he never mistook
Dr. Franklin for George Washington, or Jim Lane for Gen.
Beauregard, but invariably called every man by the name he had

given him. He once captured a stuffed figure used as a scarecrow in a cornfield, and he thought his prisoner must have been an officer of high rank from the elegant clothing of which he had deprived him, and would call attention to the fineness of the cloth and the richness of the gold lace of the rags he prized so highly.

On another occasion he took possession of a wagon full of household and kitchen furniture, but every article, in his eyes, was so magnified that he acted as if he were the owner of untold wealth; yet he was generous with his newly-found treasure, and with a stately air gave it to its real owner. Indeed, while witnessing some of his strange freaks and the deep seriousness of his manner, one could not help thinking of Don Quixote, who saw enemies in skins of wine, and fearful giants in harmless windmills.

One cold night he entered the court-house, a large brick structure, ascended the cupola, and feeling cold he built a fire which communicated to the woodwork, and cut off all means of escape. The flames soon attracted the attention of the citizens, and when they reached the public square the first thing they saw was Bill running around on the roof, crying out that the Capitol was burning, and urging them to bring the engines to save it from destruction. Soon the roof took fire, and he for the first time seemed to be aware of his own danger; he then began to call lustily for help, begged them to bring some feather-beds for him to jump down on, and when the flames pressed upon him and no other way of escape seemed possible, he seized the lightning-rod, and attempted to descend by it, but losing his hold he fell some forty or fifty feet, and was so little injured as to be walking around the next day. His account of his fall was amusing; he said he broke both his arms and his leg in three places. Some one expressed surprise that he had not broken his neck; "I did," said he, stretching it out for inspection; "but I broke it back again."

His allusions to home and the friends there, at times, were

most touching; then he would sing most plaintively, and at other times he would startle the whole town by running through the streets at midnight, uttering his frantic and maniacal howlings. His most notable exploit, however, was halting an army. It occurred as follows:

On the night of the 27th of October, 1862, Gen. Schofield was reported to be near our town; by some means Bill had heard the rumor, and prepared himself accordingly. He went out to the edge of town, and stationed himself by the roadside, and waited for the enemy. About midnight the head of the column came up, and Bill, in a commanding tone, gave the order to halt; it was obeyed, and they stood for some time in doubt, not knowing but that the order was given by authority. At last an officer asked, "Who are you?" and Bill replied, "Gen. Jim Rains." This was enough; a number of guns were leveled, a volley was fired, and Bill fell, exclaiming in most piteous tones, "O, you have killed your grandmother! you have killed your grandmother!" He was unhurt, having, perhaps, fallen as he saw the guns leveled. His exclamation revealed his true character.

Poor Bill! the last time I saw him he had broken out of the jail, in which it had become necessary to confine him, and was running as if for life; his garments, which he had torn into strings, were streaming in the wind; he was brandishing a club and shrieking as if pursued by avenging furies. I heard some time afterward that he was killed while attempting to pass the picket guard on his way back to his home in Missouri.

When day dawned we found our town in possession of a tired and hungry army; and the soldiers, thinking that they had at last got down into Dixie, began to help themselves; considering every house the dwelling of a foe, all fared alike, or, if there was any difference, the Union men a little worse than the secessionists, from the fact that the latter were far louder in their assertions of loyalty than those who had never swerved for a moment. Some who, but a few days before, would not have scrupled to assist in hanging a Union man, were now seen, hat

in hand, volunteering information to Gen. Schofield concerning the rebels under Hindman, and some of them received protection, while true men suffered. The fact was, they made
professions which it was difficult to disbelieve; while Union
men, more modest, suffered in silence; nay, if a Union man ventured to say so, relying simply upon the truth of what he said
unsupported by any extravagant assertion of loyalty, he generally received the answer, "Yes, you are all Union when we come
in," and they would proceed to help themselves to any thing
which pleased their fancy.

My yard was soon stripped of poultry, my house was filled
with soldiers, and we were feeding them as rapidly as we could;
some few of them, who had been down on a scouting party, knew
me, and their presence was valuable for a time; but other hungry
crowds came, and many of them I have no doubt thought that
they were cleaning out a secessionist, and did it with a good will;
and while I was doing my best to feed as many as the kitchen
would hold, and sending them away to have their places filled by
others, if possible hungrier still, a number went to the back part
of the smokehouse, pulled off some of the planks, and appropri-
ated every thing they could lay hands on. The door was in sight
of the kitchen, where I was engaged feeding hungry men by the
dozen, and as that was untouched I thought all safe till the sight
of men passing, every one with his hands full, arrested my attention; I went out and found the smoke-house full of men, but
stripped of every thing portable—bacon, dried-beef, salt—then
a precious article, worth a dollar a pint—saddle, bridle; in a word,
every thing gone. We had by this time exhausted nearly all we
had in the house in feeding our numerous guests, and I was soon
compelled to tell all new comers that they had come too late.
This, however, I had learned to regard as one of the unavoidable
consequences of war, and it would have been expecting too much
to suppose that a large army, just after a long night march, would
have conducted themselves with as much propriety as a caravan
of peaceful emigrants on their way to the West. They were in an

enemy's country, their supply-wagons were not always in reach, their necessities were pressing, and there was neither time nor inclination for discussing the rights of property; they had learned, too, that every man who had any thing to lose, almost invariably became a Union man on their approach; and had they respected the rights of every man who claimed to be loyal, many of them would have gone hungry much longer than would have been agreeable; moreover, I had learned that hungry men were not to be reasoned with, and learned to look upon the losses I sustained as the inevitable results of war; and I can well remember having stood by camp-fires made from the fence around my own residence, and held conversations really agreeable with the soldiers who had taken them for that purpose, and I truly felt that it would have been expecting too much from men, cold and weary, to go seek and cut fuel after the day's march, when my fence was so near. Had a party of travelers two years before done the same thing, I should, in common with all others, have deemed it a great outrage; but in the case above referred to, although I was the sufferer, I did not feel that it was so grievous a wrong; it was one of the inevitable evils which war inflicts on friends and foes alike; hence I did not then, nor do I now, complain.

This was the first large and well-appointed Union army we had seen. We were given to understand that it was the intention to hold the country, and we felt no doubt of the ability of such an army to do so. Not far behind this army was my friend Tebbetts, who, for months, had been separated from his family, and now, united with them once more, they determined not to sever again. Again, however, we were doomed to disappointment; after a stay of two or three days the order was given for the army to fall back, and many determined to leave with the troops. My friend, before mentioned, and his family, the family of Elder Graham, who, some months before, had made his escape through the Southern lines, and a number of others were among the number; besides these there was quite an exodus among the blacks; some of those who had disappeared very mysteriously, before the troops came in, were visible again, and gladly took up their march toward the north star; and when the retreating army and the cavalcade by which it was accompanied disappeared from view I felt almost alone. Nearly every one to whom I could speak unreservedly had now gone, and the days now seemed longer far than ever before. My little school, which had been such a solace, was broken up, but few of the members of the Church to which I ministered remained, and our devoted region seemed given over to the tender mercies of Hindman and the Confederacy.

Thus passed several weeks, and terrible weeks they were; anxious days and sleepless nights succeeded each other; many nights were passed in watching; sometimes our little ones would start from their sleep and look upon us, as we sat silent by the fire, with a puzzled, pained look that was most distressing, and without a word would sink again to uneasy slumbers. Indeed, those weeks seemed like one long weary night; sad and slow were the hours, haunted by painful forebodings, as if by evil dreams; but, thank God, that night had an end, and the morning came at last. That morning, reader, was ushered in by the decisive victory at Prairie Grove.

On the evening of the 6th of December, when I reached home, I found a cavalry-man with drawn saber standing at my gate, and learned from him that he belonged to the advance guard of Gen. Herron's army, who had given orders to guard every house in the place, so that no citizen might be disturbed as the main body of the army passed through. In a few minutes every house in the line of march was similarly protected, and many heart-felt thanks were expressed for the considerate care manifested by this young and gallant General. Soon his cavalry swept through town in haste to reënforce Gen. Blunt, who had routed a body of the enemy a few days before, and was now threatened by a large force under Gen. Hindman, and succeeded before daylight in effecting a junction with him. About midnight the infantry came up, having marched one hundred miles

in three days and nights—one of the hardest forced marches
of the war. They were halted in town for a few hours, and so
exhausted were they that many were asleep in a few moments
after the halt was ordered. Others seized any thing and every
thing that was combustible—fences, outbuildings, whatever
came to hand—and soon hundreds of camp-fires were blazing,
and an army reposing around them. He would have been heart-
less, indeed, who could have called that wanton destruction,
which indeed looked like it, when the wants of those brave fellows and their long and fatiguing march were remembered. As
it was, I for one, at least, looked upon the scene with pleasure
rather than regret. Several of the tired men came into my house,
and soon, stretched out before the fire, became forgetful of the
toils of the march. One there was that I well remember, a bright,
intelligent youth, a bugler in the 1st Iowa Cavalry; he had left
College to serve his country, had been very ill, and was unfit for
such a march. A cup of tea and a little food revived him; we
soon became well acquainted, and not an hour had elapsed
before he was in a calm and untroubled sleep, evidently feeling
as safe as if under the roof of his distant home. In a few hours
the bugle sounded, and all started to their feet, our young friend
much refreshed; soon all of them to mingle in the din and roar
of battle.

By daylight the town was deserted, but the calm and silence
of that lovely Sabbath morning were soon broken by the roar
of cannon, which told that the strife had begun; the smoke of
the battle was visible, and even the rattle of musketry at times
reached our ears. For hours the contest raged till about two in
the afternoon, when the firing slackened for a time. About four
it was renewed with greater violence than before; we knew that
the final struggle had come, but knew not at that time on which
side the advantage lay; but we learned afterward that Gen.
Herron, with six regiments of infantry and a small cavalry
support, had held the field all the day long against the vastly-
superior forces of Hindman, but at the hour above mentioned

Blunt arrived, and the contest raged for a short time with redoubled fury. The few Union families remaining were greatly excited during the day; a fearful battle was raging in hearing, nay, almost in sight; the Union army was in the heart of an enemy's country, and if defeated there was little hope of its escape, and in case of a retreat it was fully expected that there would be a running fight through the town; in which event all the hopes we had entertained of deliverance from secession sway would be crushed. When the sounds of battle ceased our anxiety was not relieved; we knew the conflict was over, but knew not yet whether the brave little band, which had marched by ere the sun of that day had risen, were victors or vanquished. About midnight two men from a cavalry regiment which was in the advance in the morning, came to my house and reported that their regiment had been surprised by the enemy under Marmaduke; that their train was captured, and many of their companions taken prisoners; that they had escaped on foot, and supposed that the day had gone against the Federal forces.

The next morning came, and the first sight that met my eyes was calculated to confirm my worst fears. I saw down the street several pieces of artillery, and the heads of the horses which drew them were turned northward, and my heart sank within me as I saw the proof, as I then deemed it, of disaster and retreat. But my gloom was soon turned to gladness; I hurried down and found that the artillery was for the defense of the town, which was to be henceforth a military post. I also learned that Herron's noble handful, wearied as they were, had nobly held their ground with the loss, in some regiments, of over one-third of their number; that the fierce renewal of the battle in the afternoon was when Blunt burst in fury upon the foe, and that by daylight Hindman, who had anticipated an easy victory, with his fleeing and broken legions was miles away, leaving his dead and wounded, and all the spoils of the field to one who proved himself as humane when the battle was over as he was brave during the long and deadly strife. The victory was decisive; the army of Hindman, broken and dispirited, was never again able to make a successful stand; his soldiers deserted him by hundreds, and the men of Illinois, Iowa, Indiana, and Wisconsin carried the flag of the Union to the Arkansas River, never to be withdrawn, and gained for themselves imperishable renown.

CHAPTER XI.

AFTER THE BATTLE.

Arrival of the wounded—The hospitals—Fortitude of the wounded—Deserters—Change of opinion—Venus and Mars, or woman's wit.

THE joy of victory, however, was soon saddened by the usual attendants of success upon the battle-field. The ambulances, with their mangled and bleeding freight, began to arrive, and groans of agony extorted by every inequality of the road over which they passed were heard. Many of the slightly wounded, supported by a friendly stick, or the stout arm of a friend, began to come in, and erelong the town was one vast hospital. Reader, have you ever had your mind fired by glowing descriptions of military glory, the stern and high delights of war? Remember, that to every picture of this kind there is a dark and fearful background; the plain strewed with dead, the living in every form of mutilation and disfigurement; strong men writhing in speechless agony, the compressed lip, and the pain-drop on the brow, alone telling what words would be powerless to tell. Add to this the thought that the mangled and bleeding sufferers are hundreds of miles from home, among strangers and even enemies, no kind voice to console, no soft hand to soothe; the lip parched, the wound burning; or the life-blood, from wounds that skill can not stanch, ebbing slowly away, and you have before you, not the romance, but the reality of war.

I believe I was the first citizen to minister to these suffering ones; as soon as they began to arrive, I went to the Female

Seminary, one of the receptacles of the wounded; there was then only one man, an officer, there. He was a large, fine-looking man; his wound was painful and dangerous, his eyes were closed, no complaint or moan escaped him; hundreds of others, as yet without shelter, rendered any aid to him at present out of the question; I laid my hand upon his brow, and asked him the nature of his wound; he started in surprise at the sound of a strange, yet kind voice—answered my inquiries—told me he was from Indianapolis; and when he learned that many whom he knew there were friends of mine, he for the time being seemed to forget his pain in his joy.

I said he was the only occupant of that large building, but when I next visited it the entire floor was so thickly covered with mangled and bleeding men that it was difficult to thread my way among them; some were mortally wounded, the life fast escaping through a ghastly hole in the breast; the limbs of others were shattered and useless, the faces of others so disfigured as to seem scarcely human; the bloody bandages, hair clotted, and garments stained with blood, and all these with but little covering, and no other couch than the straw, with which the floor was strewed, made up a scene more pitiable and horrible than I had ever conceived possible before. Nor was this the only place which presented so sad a spectacle; it was repeated in about twenty other buildings, including the various churches, all of which were thronged with the sad wrecks of humanity from that field which in song and story will long be remembered as Prairie Grove.

Sad, however, as was the scene in the hospital to which I have alluded, it was exceeded, perhaps, by the force of contrast in the church, in which I was accustomed to minister; the seats were removed, and the entire floor covered with bleeding and mangled men; and when I thought of the throngs which had often gathered there for worship, and looked upon the scene then presented, the contrast was most painful. The number of wounded was so great, and supplies so scanty, that for a few days the little I was able to furnish them seemed luxurious when compared with the coarse fare with which they were served; but a few days made a great change for the better; supplies began to come in—the Sanitary Commission was well represented; and Gov. Morton, as soon as he heard that a regiment from his State had suffered severely in the fight, lost no time in sending such aid as was needed. Many and warm were the blessings upon his name by the wounded of the twenty-sixth Indiana, who to a man regarded him as the soldiers' friend, for to them, far away on the frontier, the evidences of his care were most grateful, and will be long remembered.

During the first few days after the battle many of the severely wounded died; and to me it was a sad sight when, for the first time, I saw a corpse, stark and cold, laid outside of the hospital upon the ground, with no covering but a blanket or overcoat, soon to be carried away by the dozen to nameless graves. Hitherto I had cherished great reverence for the human body, even after the spirit had departed; and to see the bodies of men treated with as little ceremony as is wont to be bestowed upon brutes, was sad in the extreme. My heart sickened, too, when I saw, for the first time, the surgeons carving and sawing the limbs of men like butchers in the shambles; and yet I soon learned that their very coolness was a mercy; there was no time for weakness; that would unnerve the skillful hand when the lives of so many were depending upon their promptness and energy; and indeed it was not long before I could myself stand by the side of one undergoing amputation, and soothe him in the trying ordeal which at first to witness unmanned me.

Among those who had to pass the terrible ordeal of losing a limb was a rebel soldier, for the wounded, whether friends or foes, were all cared for in turn; he had a pleasing face, and an eye mild, soft, and tender as a woman's. I was attracted to him the moment I saw him, and his voice and manner fully corresponded with his looks; his wound was a fearful one, and he scarcely expected to survive the necessary operation. I stood by him in his hour of trial; he bore it uncomplainingly, but the shock was too great, and he sunk from the loss of blood, and his friends to this hour perhaps are ignorant of his sad fate.

I must say, however, that the wounded bore their sufferings like the heroes that they were; no abandonment to grief or use-less complaining, but on the contrary, many were calm, and some even cheerful. One noble fellow I well remember; a ball had passed laterally through his breast, a horrible wound, rendering his breathing difficult and painful; the bright red blood, which every feeble cough brought into his mouth, showed that his lungs had been pierced, and yet he was hopeful and cheerful. "I know," said he, "that it is an ugly wound, but I am not going to make a poor mouth about it; I will keep up a good heart, come what may." And he did keep up a stout heart, and I had the pleasure of seeing him on his feet and able to march again. Indeed, among the hundreds that I saw almost daily, I heard no weak and unmanly complaints. The calm endurance of some, and the eagerness of others for another encounter with the foe as soon as fit for service, was a matter for wonder, and afforded quite a marked contrast to what I had witnessed, months before in the same place, on the part of sick and wounded Confederate sol-diers, whose only language was that of complaint, their only long-ing, for home. Poor fellows! many of them were found in the ranks against their own will; hence their desire for the homes they had left so unwillingly.

It was not long, however, before the condition of those in the hospitals was greatly improved; no pains were spared to ren-der them comfortable; abundant supplies of all kinds soon arrived, and all that skill and kindness could do was exerted for their comfort, and the poor sufferers themselves said that it was next to being at home. I still continued my visits almost daily, and it is yet a gratification to think that I made many hours seem less weary than they otherwise would have been, and I learned many a sad, and many a profitable lesson, unknown in the days of peace. I had a patient also at home, a young man who was brought to my house, the day after the battle, with the delirium of fever upon him, and, as we thought, not far from his end; but we had the gratification of seeing him slowly improve, and at last he was able to rejoin his regiment. Soldiers are thought to be, in the main, rude, coarse men; if not so at first, rendered so by their profession; but never, in my intercourse with men, have I found warmer hearts or deeper gratitude than was manifested by those men, tried on many a hard-fought field, for any little service that I was able to render them. And after the scenes of sorrow and suffering which those weeks brought under my notice, the fortitude and true manhood which they also disclosed gave me a higher opinion of my race than I had ever entertained before.

Among those who fell in the rebel ranks were two young men of our town; the parents of one and the mother of the other were members of my congregation. Their bodies were brought home for interment, and it was sad to look on their noble forms both pierced through the heart by the messengers of death; and it was sad beyond expression to witness the agony of a mother's heart as she kissed again and again the cold lips of her proud boy, her first-born, as she clung to his lifeless form, refusing almost to be separated by death.

Then the scene changed; many who had been forced into the rebel ranks took the opportunity which the battle and defeat gave them to abandon the cause for which they had never willingly struck a blow; and the sincerity of many was evinced by immediately enlisting in the National service; and the Union never had braver or truer men to bear arms in its defense than many of those who but a few days before were in the ranks of its foes—there, because, in many instances, they had the choice between that and, not a soldier's but a felon's, death. It is easy for those, who have never been tried, to boast how, like martyrs, they would have died before they would have been found in the rebel ranks; but these men did better than to fling their lives uselessly away by yielding to a necessity that it would have

been madness to resist, and, as soon as the moment came, per-
iling their lives for the flag and the cause which had ever been
dearest to their hearts.

The state of affairs was now greatly changed; Union men
who had been compelled to flee for their lives returned, nearly
all the secessionists had disappeared, and the few who remained
were either loud in their professions of loyalty, or most eagerly
courting the good offices of Union men in their behalf. Our
once peaceful College grove was converted into a camp for the
tenth Regiment Illinois Cavalry; large supply trains came in;
the flavor of genuine coffee was known again by many to whom
it had long been a matter of pleasant recollection, and many
families were fed by that very Government which their brothers, husbands, and sons were madly endeavoring to destroy.
Even many of the ladies, who had hitherto been unable to
express their intense hatred of the Yankees, soon made the discovery, and indeed were not slow to express it, that they were
gentlemen, and treated them as if they actually believed it.
Wounded officers were quartered in nearly every house, and
some who when they received them would barely admit that
they were of the same race with themselves, were fully per-
suaded before they left, that the North had its noblemen as well
as the South. Indeed, when the comparison was made between
the soldiers of both sides which had alternately occupied our
town, the result was not unfavorable to the men who upheld
the flag of the Union. And Southerners who had witnessed
the arrogance of Hindman, could not help admiring the noble,
gentlemanly courtesy of his youthful and brave conqueror, Gen.
Frank Herron.

But there were other scenes and incidents than those in
which blood and tears so often and freely mingled; like the shift-
ing scenes of a drama, they came with the added charm of reality and truth. Our town had become a military post, and the
commandant was one whose kindness of heart will long be
remembered. He was a man in middle life, whom position had

not rendered arrogant; the head of a family, which made him feel for suffering families, even in an enemy's country; pleasant and affable to all, he conciliated many whom harshness would have confirmed in the disloyalty which was the fashion, where it was not so from any real love of the rebellion. There were ladies who were pleased at being esteemed intensely Southern, when their interests, and in some cases their husbands, were on the Union side; and yet, for what reason I could never divine, they took great pleasure in saying piquant and even annoying things to the Union officers, whom courtesy prevented from giving such replies as truth would have warranted. This was the case even in families who were indebted to the kindness of these very officers, not only for protection from annoyance or insult, but even for fuel and provisions; the former being brought to their doors by army wagons, the latter stores drawn from the commissary department, and such as had not been known in that region for months.

Colonel W. boarded at the house of one of these ladies, who, possessed of fine conversational powers and a keen wit, managed to say things which, though accompanied by a smile or wicked, ringing laugh, nevertheless made the young officers, whom business brought down to the Colonel's room, to feel quite unpleasant. The Colonel himself was never made to feel so in the least degree; his kind, unobtrusive goodness had won upon the feelings of his hostess; his kindness was fully appreciated, and she knew that in him she had a protector and friend. Her husband was in the rebel army, and yet his position was far from being one of choice; he had kept out as long as possible, and his entering the service was looked upon as a matter of necessity. Colonel W. had learned that her husband was not a very dangerous rebel, and probably had made the discovery that his hostess was at heart not so disloyal as she seemed anxious for some to think, and acted as if he were an old friend enjoying the hospitality of the house, instead of being at once protector and provider, as he really was. While the Colonel was there, an old friend and schoolmate of his hostess was also spending some time with her, under the following circumstances: She had been married but a few months to a young gentleman of Jackson county, Mo., a man of large fortune, much of it in slaves, then a very precarious kind of property. A large number of these he had taken inside the Southern lines for safety, and was obliged to enter the army to prove that his property deserved the protection sought for it there. To try and rejoin her husband was the object of Mrs. S.'s visit. The battle of Prairie Grove had just taken place, and to obtain a pass through the lines was for a time very difficult. Mrs. S. was young, quite pleasing in appearance, well educated, possessed of a fine voice, was a good musician, and often she would make the evenings pass most pleasantly with music and song. Some old, plaintive ballads she sang most touchingly, accompanying herself on the guitar; and when she sang with great pathos "Home, Sweet Home," it would bear our good Colonel to his own dear home in the West. One evening the fair singer, who had by this time become well acquainted with him, and after having brought a mist over his eyes by her sweet, plaintive songs, said: "Colonel, I don't think I'll sing any more for you, not even 'Sweet Home,' unless you give me a pass to go through the lines and see my husband." And so well did she plead, that he consented, and ordered his Adjutant to give her a pass.

The next morning the young wife, all joy, gratitude, and smiles, was preparing to leave, and about the middle of the day, when the Colonel and his Adjutant came to dinner, they found Mrs. S. just ready to bid them farewell; her carriage was at the door, and in a few moments she expected to be on her way; she was only delaying to bid farewell to him who had so kindly granted her heart's dearest wish. But, alas! an order had just come in to the Colonel, from Gen. Herron, to permit no one under any circumstances to pass through the lines; the order was imperative, and when he informed her that she could not be permitted to go on her journey, the disappointment was so great that she burst into tears. Her hostess and friend wept with her, the Colonel had to brush away a tear; his Adjutant, a fine young officer, wept; they all wept together, and the Colonel, unable to endure the sight, with his Adjutant withdrew dinnerless. Scarcely had they got out of view when a strange light came into the eyes of Mrs. S.; her pass had been revoked, but it was still in her possession; hardly pausing to say farewell, she stepped into her carriage and gave the order to drive on. The pickets were reached, the pass proved an "open sesame," and when the Colonel came to supper, still looking sad at the disappointment of his fair friend, and not seeing her at the table, he concluded that she had not overcome her sorrow, and soon returned to his office. The next morning at breakfast he ventured the remark to his hostess that "Mrs. S. was not down this morning;" the reply was, "No." At dinner her place was still vacant, and he asked, "Where is Mrs. S.?" Imagine, if you can, his surprise when he heard the reply, "She has gone."

It was even so; armed with his pass, she had passed the pickets. He immediately ordered some mounted-men in pursuit, but she was twenty-four hours in advance of them, and knowing the danger of capture, had doubtless not spared her horses, and was then forty or fifty miles away, safe within the Southern lines.

Of course the pursuit was fruitless, and I do not think that the Colonel regarded the fugitive as a very dangerous rebel; indeed, when the escape was the subject of remark, there was a subdued smile on the face, and the least twinkle in the eye, which spoke of any thing but chagrin or regret. Of Mrs. S. we never heard again, but, doubtless, she met, as she deserved, the husband she risked so much to rejoin.

CHAPTER XII.

PEN PORTRAITS.

Changed scenes—The fickle—The bold—A Confederate officer—Veterans—The patriot—The major—A new convert—The true man—The recreant—A hero—Last-ditch men.

THE comparative quiet which we now enjoyed afforded an opportunity for noting the changes which two years of war had effected. Many of our youth had fallen in battle, others had died in the camp or hospital. Many of our best citizens had gone North, while others had removed still further South; indeed, I might say, few remained who had the means of getting away. Our population was larger than ever, but composed in a great measure of strangers; convalescents from the different hospitals might be seen at every turn; we had a regiment of loyal Arkansians encamped with us; and their families, from whom they had long been separated, thronged in from various parts of the country to see them. Men who had reached threescore, whose lives had hitherto been not only peaceful, but religious, maddened by outrages which had been inflicted upon their families, whom they had been compelled to abandon to save their own lives, were now to be found in uniform, and with arms in their hands, seeking redress for the wrongs they had endured; and young men, burning to avenge injuries inflicted upon aged parents, were daily entering the ranks. Refugees from Texas came with their tales of suffering; repentant rebels thronged the office of the Provost Marshal to take the oath of allegiance. The regimental band refreshed our ears nightly with National airs, which had long been proscribed; letters and newspapers made their appearance once more. Wagons, laden with goods to supply wants that had become very pressing, came down from Missouri, and as there was quite a prospect of gain, there came the inevitable, the wandering Jew.

Nor was it a study devoid of interest to note in the crowd the marked difference which the trials of the past two years had made in the characters of some well-known citizens who yet remained. In some the ordeal had developed traits most honorable, in others disclosed defects, the very existence of which had hitherto been unsuspected. As the same fire which consumes the dross purifies the gold, and as the same sun melts wax and hardens clay, so do the same trials exalt some men while they only serve to debase others.

A few of these cases, drawn from life, we will present before the reader. Here is one whose very walk indicates the greatest timidity, so desirous of being on the right, that is, the successful side, that he could not tell which side he was on till he had heard the latest news; he was ever wavering, not knowing but that his position of to-day might be destroyed by the news of to-morrow. If he fell in with a sanguine Union man in the morning, he was likely to be one himself for that day at least; but if a secessionist made sundry mysterious predictions in a manner which seemed to indicate that he knew much more than he cared to tell, it was more than likely that he would protest that he always thought the South would conquer. No man rejoiced more at a Union victory; but was also glad at a Confederate success; and had he known beyond a peradventure which side would eventually succeed, his own position would not have been doubtful.

Very different is that large, heavy, slow-moving man, who, though silent now that the Federals are here, never failed before their coming to express his opinions very freely, and who never changed them after they were expressed. He was an open and avowed secessionist; his utterances were oracular; he seemed rather to know than to believe whatever he told. Others might have misgivings with regard to news and rumors, he had none; yet he had no bitter feelings toward Union men; he never threatened, never brandished knife, or took up gun. Nearly all others on his side, when they heard the Federals were coming, would flee as if for life, but he never seemed disturbed at their approach; all the effect their coming seemed to have on him was to make him stop "secesh talk" while they remained; he never talked on the other side. He had, in a word, all the noise of secession without its intolerant spirit. By some means he kept on friendly terms with all. Though in favor of the Confederacy, you could not persuade him to have much to do with Confederate money; he would take it when he saw a way for getting rid of it again very speedily, but ordinarily he would prefer a man's note to payment in Confederate notes. He would, and did, lend Union men money, and that, too, in gold, and would wait any length of time rather than receive the current paper, even at a heavy discount, in payment. Had all secessionists been of his type, there would have been no rebellion.

That is an officer in the Confederate army; he is here with a flag of truce to effect an exchange of prisoners; he is yet young; his bronzed cheek is not due to exposure alone, but in a measure to his Indian blood. Approach him and you will soon find that he has all the ease and courtesy of a true gentleman; he is gifted, too, as both eye and face unmistakably declare. But he is a rebel—yes; but not one of the proud, ignorant despisers of the men of the North, who think that Southern men are born to be masters, and that all others have the spirit of serfs. No; he was educated in New England, and he can never forget the lessons learned there. Before the war broke out he was a rising man, and though identified with the rebellion, no one can say that he strove to bring it about; nay, he long resisted the idea of separation, and when the State was linked to the Confederacy he went with her in sorrow. But mark him; even now no Union man avoids him, nor is there a shade of distrust on his frank face when he meets them. Not one of them thinks him a rebel at heart, nor does he think any the less of his old friends because of their loyalty. He yielded to a false principle, but he has not a bad heart; and could the secrets of that heart be read, few doubt that a love of the Union would be found there still. Union men would be glad to have him stand with them, but since that may not be so, they wish that all their enemies were as free from personal bitterness, and as incapable of cruelty even to a foe as he.

Here are two others, aged men, veterans of the late war; they had maintained the honor of their country's flag against the power of Great Britain, they had witnessed its triumph, and they were not the men to desert it now. O, how their voices trembled with emotion when they spoke of the victories achieved under its glorious folds! how their hearts throbbed, and the light of other days flashed from their eyes when they found themselves under that flag of the free once more! These men commanded the respect even of secessionists. Before strong hands brought back the flag they felt they could not expect them to be faithless to the deeds and memories of the past; and while their lips wel-comed men of the North and West who espoused the cause of the South, their hearts paid a silent tribute to the unwavering patriotism of those noble old men.

That man, past middle-age, slightly built, mild of speech, and unobtrusive in manners, yet with a look of unconquerable resolution, is Isaac Murphy, who, when the Convention, under the influence of threats, promises, falsehood, and the spirit of madness that ruled the hour, voted for the Ordinance of Secession, alone dared to stand up in his place and thunder "No!"—who, when appealed to by recreant Union men to make the vote unanimous by yielding like them, still stood firm; and when threatened with death by traitors said, "You may drive the steel through my heart, but I will never vote for your accursed Ordinance."

Don't mistake this young man for a Federal, although dressed in the true blue. That coat was obtained in Mississippi, where there was no choice, at a great price, and the wearer has the rank of Major in the Confederate service; don't be alarmed, he is no spy, nor is he a prisoner. Don't think that I am compromised by being in company with him; he graduated at our College years ago, and, just before the war broke out, had the degree of A. M. conferred upon him. He has a furlough from Gen. Pemberton in his pocket, and I am on my way to give him an introduction to Col. Wickersham; and the interview ends by his taking the oath and returning to his allegiance. He has been in the North as a prisoner of war; has found that the charges made by Southern leaders are unwarranted; that on the one side it is a war for human rights, on the other, to perpetuate slavery; he is convinced of his error, and wishes to abandon a cause he no longer regards as just. His experience has been severe, but the cure is complete. To-morrow he will rejoin his wife, from whom he has been long parted, and together they will seek a home in the North.

Engaged yonder in conversation with several Federal officers, and evidently entertaining them, is one of our citizens, whom a stranger would be apt to set down as nobly loyal. He can give more information concerning the rebels than any man in town, and, indeed, is not slow to offer it. His manner is affable and courteous, he has a pleasant word and smile for all, but he is not what he seems; he has hitherto been a secessionist, and an intolerant one, and it would doubtless confuse him somewhat were a Union man to step up and tell of one who formerly flourished a very formidable Bowie knife, and talked loudly of extermination, who thought no epithet too coarse, no abuse too vile for those who refused to attempt the destruction of a Government under which they had enjoyed such manifold blessings, and then were to close by saying, "Thou art the man!"

All this he was, and more; yet he never placed himself in peril, though ready to imperil others; a boaster, yet no act of his showed him brave; and now, when those he had so loudly denounced had come to restore the rights of the people, none seemed to give them a more cordial welcome than he. Union men, who had been overawed by him and such as he, nobly were silent concerning the past, and that silence, he must have felt, was as generous on their part as it was undeserved on his own. Had the change been less sudden, it might have been deemed the result of conviction; but conversions like his are more frequently from policy than from principle.

If there be any truth in looks, that is an honest face; it is that of a man well advanced in years, but still vigorous; he has just discovered quite a large number of guns hidden by some zealous Confederate, without his knowledge, in one of his outbuildings, and has reported the matter to the Provost Marshal. The fact, in itself a suspicious one, is fully explained by his frank statement, but building and arms are soon destroyed by the military authorities. Had the arms been found there before he himself discovered them, explanation would have been difficult in the face of the facts; yet he makes no effort to find out the neighbor who had placed him in such peril by putting him, seemingly, in an attitude of hostility to a Government to which he was unalterably attached. To have learned the facts and pointed out the true author of the deed would not have been difficult, and perhaps the neighbor, unworthy of the name, trembled when they met face to face; but he was in no danger—the old man had learned from the Bible the precept to return good for evil, and acted upon it. He was one of the few whose religion stood the test of those times of trial; friend and enemy were alike to him if in need, and he had learned the difficult lesson to suffer uncomplainingly at the hands of professed friends and open foes. He performed many a quiet deed of mercy at a time when selfishness was exalted almost into a virtue, under circumstances which proved that he looked to God alone for his reward.

The next picture is different. It is a man past middle age, clad in a military coat, which rumor said was among the first spoils seized by secessionists when they laid hands on all United States' property that could be found. Be that as it may, under that blue covering there beats no loyal heart. He was a Western man, and had spent but a few years in the South; and though he had but little visible interest there, with what seemed to many of us a strange perversity, he was most clamorous for rights, which in his case, at least, had never been disturbed. By reason of age, beyond the reach of the conscript law, he nevertheless took up his gun and marched against the men of the very State in which he had spent the best years of his life. He had accompanied the rebels in their flight southward, but had returned; and as his coat seemed to indicate more love for the Union than the Confederate cause, none, save a few of the people of the town, knew that he had ever taken up arms. To have heard him urging his claims for payment for rails burnt by the troops, one would have thought that he was a most loyal and deeply-injured man; while the fact was, to the utmost of his ability he had attempted to destroy the Government from which he was claiming indemnity. Nay, he was at that very time secretly cheering the drooping spirits of secessionists, by hopes of a speedy advance of the Confederate army; recreant to all his past history without any perceptible cause, and certainly without any justification. Nor did he stand alone; several free-State men identified themselves with the rebellion, and went to even greater extremes than men whose feet had never touched free soil. The motives which led them to pursue this course I was not able to discover; they had not even the poor motive of property to influence them, and yet to other Union men they were in some instances a greater terror than men of Southern birth. I said they were feared; they had given the lie to their previous lives, early training, and associations; by their new friends they were received seemingly with open arms, but with real distrust; by their former friends, who were still true, if feared they were also scorned.

In the office of the Provost Marshal, preparing copies of the oath of allegiance, is a gray-haired man, slightly bent with age, whose conduct had ever been the opposite of that we have just noticed; he had from the first denounced the rebellion, and predicted its utter failure. Several disguised Confederate soldiers, representing themselves as Federals, one night came and sought to entrap him, by endeavoring to obtain from him information prejudicial to the South. They failed in their purpose, but arrested him and hurried him to camp, thence to Fort Smith, and finally to prison at Little Rock. After suffering for months he was released, and he made his way again to the Federal lines, aged, poor, suffering, but, amid all, true—an honest man, a tried patriot, a hero in humble life, but none the less a hero.

We had, moreover, more than one frightened boaster— "last-ditch men," who always had a dozen good reasons for not being in the army; these, when our town was occupied by the Union troops, put Union men to the blush by their ardent professions of loyalty, and almost made some of the officers doubt whether their own patriotism was sufficiently strong; yet they trembled while they boasted, lest some one should let out the fearful secret that they had boasted louder, if possible, on the other side. By such the oath was regarded as worse than death, before the trial came, but now, so far from being at all objectionable, it was voluntarily sought and swallowed; and some of the meekest men that I ever saw were those whose words a few weeks before were most bold and defiant; nay, they would even call upon Union men to bear witness that they had ever been in favor of the Government; and who could have the heart to expose such fear-stricken souls, who had never been bold, save in words only?

CHAPTER XIII.

PREPARING TO LEAVE.

Desolation—Removal necessary—Battle near my house
—Reasons for delay—Southern bitterness not general—The
future of the South.

THE time now began to pass wearily. Many of the wounded
had recovered sufficiently to rejoin their respective regiments,
and many, alas! had found a resting-place in the grave. The
monotony was only broken by the arrival of a supply train, or
perchance the departure or return of a scouting party, we
became as much accustomed to the sound of the bugle as we
had been in years past to that of the College bell, and the clank
of sabers became as familiar as the hammer on the anvil or any
of the sounds of peaceful life had been. Sad, sad, however, was
the change in our once beautiful and prosperous inland city; the
fences had nearly all disappeared, shrubbery and fruit-trees were
ruined, houses were deserted, nearly all the domestic animals
killed, dead cavalry-horses lay here and there; the farms, for
miles around, were laid waste, the fences having been used to
keep up the hundreds of campfires which were seldom permitted to go out by night or day; stables were pulled down, outbuildings burnt, and the very spirit of destruction seemed to rule
the hour. The contrast drawn between now and better days was
most painful; all that was once valued was destroyed or defaced,
and, worse than all, the future seemed to have no promise. The
great and decisive battles of the war had not then been fought;
the progress of the war seemed slow indeed, comparatively

little of the revolted territory had been won back; instead of being near its close the contest seemed scarcely begun.

Hitherto my life had been an active one, my duties in the College and Church had given me ample occupation, but the one was now in ruins and the other a hospital; and though I had enough to engross all my time for the first few weeks after the battle, the death of the severely wounded and the recovery of those slightly injured, together with the arrival of the Sanitary Commission train, and additional physicians, rendered my labors less necessary. No field for useful labor presented itself, the hope of saving any thing from the wreck had long since departed, and I began to look around for a place of usefulness, safety, and rest. True, there were troops stationed in our town, but the number was few, often not amounting to over three hundred, in consequence of large details for scouting parties and guarding trains; a rebel raid on a large scale, under Marmaduke, had been made north of us into Missouri, and great fears were entertained that a similar one would soon sweep through our region. I had pursued my labors as minister and teacher long after all others had abandoned them, and I felt my work there was done. True there were a few faithful ones of the flock to which I had ministered, and yet I felt that necessity must soon compel even these to leave, as the means of living were becoming more limited daily; few farmers would attempt to raise a crop in such an unsettled state of affairs, the mills were nearly all destroyed, and the food question was fast becoming one that engrossed the attention of all—one, too, which none could solve satisfactorily.

In these matters my fears were not causeless, as subsequent events proved; for not very long after my departure a rebel force of near three thousand assailed the town, and a battle raged round my dwelling, and in sight of it men lay dead and dying. My house, being in full range of the enemy's fire, suffered from their cannonade, and I doubtless left none too soon for the safety of my family. The house which I formerly occupied near the College was seized and held for a time by the enemy, and was struck and pierced by more than fifty shot, shell, and bullets. It was occupied by a large family, mainly women and children, who were adherents of the Southern cause; and when the only man who remained with them for protection entreated the officer in command at that point to withdraw his troops, so as not to endanger the women and children, the ruffian drew his revolver and shot him through the head. The fear-stricken family had all sought refuge in the cellar. A bomb-shell penetrated to the place of their retreat, but providentially did not explode, or the loss of life must have been fearful. It was, and ever will be, a sad thought to me that this battle raged over the graves of my two children, and that the little mound, which covered the dust so precious to me, was doubtless trampled and defaced by that fierce soldiery. So dear, so hallowed was that spot to me that I can not think of its sanctity being invaded by the fierce struggle which took place above where they sleep, without a sadness which words can not express.

Another circumstance hastened my departure. While those in command treated me with a kindness that I never can forget, there were some of the soldiers whose conduct rendered my position any thing but agreeable; I had looked on quietly, and without complaint, at the destruction of my property, when the circumstances were such as to render it necessary for the comfort of men on the march, and had seen wagon-load after wagon-load of my fences taken as fuel for the hospitals; but after affairs became more settled, it was far from agreeable to have my property destroyed wantonly by those who were sent, not to oppress and impoverish, but to defend all loyal men. It is true, I could have had the perpetrators of such acts punished, but I well knew that such a course would only gain the ill-will of the soldiers; hence I bore many acts of spoliation without complaint. Indeed, I had protection papers from the commandant of the post, and a safeguard from Gen. Schofield's own hand, the forcing or violation of which was death; yet, taking into consideration that those who did me injury were not aware of my true standing, and finding me in an enemy's country, took the liberty of treating me as one, I forebore to report them. One day, observing two soldiers tearing down the fence which inclosed my dwelling, I went out and told them that my property was protected by papers granted by those in authority. I had left them and was returning to the house, not a hundred yards distant, when I was met by an officer, who asked me if I had been forbidding the soldiers to destroy my fence? I told him I had; upon which, with an oath, he clutched me by the beard and drew his revolver, swearing he would blow the top of my head off. Although I felt the steel barrel touching my head, I was so taken by surprise, that I was not conscious of any very great alarm, while the ruffian still held me by the beard pouring out threats and curses. I told him that he was certainly mistaken concerning me, and offered to convince him if he would only go with me to his superior officer, who knew me well; he swore that he knew me, and would kill me; and I stood passive in his hands, feeling assured that any attempt at resistance or escape would only secure my instant destruction. My calmness seemed to have some effect upon him, and he reversed his pistol, holding it by the barrel ready to strike me if I made any resistance; he cursed me for a rebel, the only man, friend or foe, who had ever bestowed the name upon me; I offered to show him that his superior officers did not so consider me, if he would only accompany me to the house and examine the papers to which I have alluded. Finally he released me; but the moment I entered my door, and saw my wife and two little children, and thought of my narrow escape, and the helpless condition they would have been left in had the wretch executed his threat, I trembled in every limb, and realized how near to death I had been. The perpetrator of this outrage was a lieutenant, wearing the Federal uniform, and I felt far different feelings from those I experienced when in danger from Ben M'Culloch; for that I was in a measure prepared; but the other coming from a quarter from which I had a right to look for protection was the worse for being so unexpected, as well as undeserved. I have no doubt that I could have had him severely punished had I lodged my complaint at Head-Quarters, as I was urged to do by a few friends to whom I had mentioned the circumstance; but I thought the men of his command might regard him as unjustly treated, and revenge themselves upon myself, family, and property, and so I let the matter pass, intending to leave as soon as practicable. I must confess, however, to a certain degree of satisfaction, when a few months after, in reading an account of a battle in which this same officer was engaged, to find the following notice of my persecutor: "Fled ingloriously from the field Lieut. ————," while his comrades stood their ground against a vastly-superior force, and in the end routed the foe. For this cowardly conduct in the face of the enemy, I have since learned that he has met his just deserts by being disgracefully dismissed from the service. After this occurrence my family was extremely anxious that we should leave; I had escaped the scouts of Ben M'Culloch, and the plots of enemies, and now that this last imminent danger had passed, it was like tempting Providence to remain longer, and I decided to seek, if not a home, at least a refuge, in some peaceful land.

My own reasons for having remained thus long, I am well assured, will be a solution of the strange fact—to many—of so many Union men remaining in the South. Like myself, many of them had no relatives in the North with whom to seek a temporary shelter; there, too, our money would be worthless; to attempt a removal by private conveyance exposed one to almost certain robbery, and perhaps death, at the hands of guerrillas, by whom the roads were beset; and to leave a home once pleasant, though now surrounded by dangers, and to begin life anew among strangers doubtless deterred thousands from the step I had been so reluctant, but now felt compelled, to take. In addition to all these were other reasons of a more general character by which, nevertheless, the actions of men have ever been influenced.

The dwellers in the plains of Italy are loth to leave their own lovely land, and even the hardy mountaineer pines with heart and homesickness when far away from Switzerland. Think it not strange, then, that thousands in the South have been, and are yet unwilling to leave a land fairer than Italy and as picturesque as Switzerland. There are not more glorious sunsets nor more gorgeous, golden dawns along the shores of the Mediterranean, than are seen on the coasts of the Mexican Gulf. The Valley of the Nile can not boast a greater fertility than that of the Mississippi, and grander and more diversified scenes seldom meet the eye of the traveler in any land than those which are seen in the mountain regions of Arkansas. Further south the fig and orange are found, but there the fruits of the North are found in higher perfection than in any of the older States. The rigor of Winter is unknown; in February the peach-trees are in full bloom, and March there has often the beauty of May. A more salubrious climate would be difficult to find, and hundreds of the soldiers of the Army of the Frontier were surprised and delighted at the difference between the climate in Arkansas and the various States from which they came; and it was not uncommon to hear them say that when the war was over they would make it their home. Indeed, the advantages of the South were never fully appreciated before, and one of the results of the war will be that thousands, who have gone there in arms, will at no distant day throng thither to cultivate the arts of peace.

No wonder, then, that so many were unwilling to leave so desirable a country; no wonder that so many remain there still, in the hope that they may yet enjoy sweet rest in a land that to them is lovelier than any upon which the sun bestows his smile.

You never hear the poor refugee disparaging the State he has been compelled to flee; no, there still

> "Every prospect pleases,
> And only *man* is vile."

The state of society has changed; but the rich valleys and broad rivers, the mountains, the prairies, the genial climate, all the natural beauties and blessings which God bestowed are dear to him still. But it may be objected that such is the bitterness which the war has developed, that it will forever be impossible for the asperities of the present to be so far forgotten as to admit of the return of the refugee, or of any great emigration from the North and the West. Judging from the tone of the Richmond papers one would suppose this to be true; but they are not the exponents of the views of the great masses of Southern people. The tone of superiority in which they indulge is thought to be an ill-concealed contempt for the people of the North, cherished, indeed, before the war, but never expressed till now. Those, however, who have lived long enough in both sections to form a correct judgment in this matter, are well aware that such is not the case; but that, on the contrary, Northern skill, industry, talent, genius, intelligence, and virtue were never more highly appreciated and honored, even at home, than by the great majority of the Southern people.

Some few there were who affected to despise the people of the North, but it was affectation only, and a class of facts, that no one can deny, exists to prove that I am correct in what I have stated. Prior to the war the "Southern Literary Messenger" was deemed the ablest serial in the South, and yet the finest articles which appeared in it were from Northern pens. But it was not in this department alone that the impress of Northern mind was to be seen; it was felt and gratefully acknowledged in all noble and honorable pursuits.

Some years before the war, in the presence of a large audience in the State of Mississippi, the writer put forth the following as facts, which he scarcely would have ventured to do unless they had been well known to be such; they were not only tolerated, but highly approved, and a large subscription to an educational enterprise which he was advocating was the result. The portion of the address referred to is as follows: "What do we get from the North? The ax to level the forest, the plow to turn the furrow, the horse and mule to make it available, the stout brogan and the patent-leather shoe, the lady's bonnet and the gentleman's beaver; from thence come many of our fabrics of cotton, wool, flax, and hemp; nearly every good's-box, pork and flour-barrel bears a Northern brand. Wine, made from grapes grown in Ohio, sparkles in the rich man's glass; and from up the river, too, comes the loafer's whisky. Your horse knows the flavor of Northern oats, and the planter's wife and daughters roll to church in a Northern carriage. Hogs raised in a colder clime give the sugar-cured ham that graces the head of your table, and the same animal furnishes the light by which you read the Picayune and Delta. Boston sends crackers, New York sends butter, and the Western Reserve cheese by the tun. From the same point of the compass come the soap for shaving, the blacking for your boots; and the very match with which you light your cigar. Nay, I am not certain but that you sleep on a Northern bed, have your dinner cooked on a stove which hails from the same direction; so with the furniture of your parlor, and the carpet on your floor, and even music floats to your ear from instruments fashioned by Northern hands. Almost every thing we eat, drink, wear, and read has the same history; the ink in these words, the pen with which I have traced them, and the paper on which I write, all came from the North. But this is not all; we get from the North our education, our educators, and our professional men. A Northern physician must bleed or blister you, as the case may be; your cause must be pleaded by a Northern tongue, your will written by a Northern hand; Northern divines fill your pulpits, Northern teachers your schools, in which you seldom find a Southern text-book. These

men from the North fill their respective places worthily and
well; they are the missionaries of science, education, and religion; tongue could not tell the present condition of the South
had they remained at home; they came from a colder clime, but
not as idlers to live on your bounty, but as benefactors to engage
in the noblest employments, by which you are much greater
gainers than they. And when the South is fully awakened to the
duty which she owes to her own children, she will find none
more zealous in assisting in the spread of intelligence, and
virtue, and all the blessings which follow in their train, than
those who have left home and kindred in the North to find a
home in this Southern land.

"Our country, too, is rapidly gaining an honorable position
in the world of letters; English reviewers can no longer sneer-
ingly ask, 'Who reads an American book?' for Bancroft, Prescott,
Irving, Bryant, and Longfellow have already achieved a wide and
honorable transatlantic reputation; and yet while we think with
pride of those Americans who have done so much to elevate our
national literature, it is by no means a pleasant reflection that
the South has done but little in this noble field, has but little
share in this bloodless yet not inglorious triumph." That language
like this was warranted by the facts is well known to every man
who has passed a few years in the South; and I have no doubt
that the bitterness which exists, like the boasting once so common, will be found to be confined to a very small class; nor do I
think the day far distant when, under the influence of Northern
industry and enterprise, the South shall abound in the elements
of prosperity and happiness to a degree unknown before. I have
been led to this disgression from the fact that great difficulty has
been anticipated where but little really exists, and I can not resist
the conviction that when the mad project of the guilty few is
thwarted, the many who have been deceived, and the many still
true, with the loyal States will form one free, happy, undivided
and indivisible people.

CHAPTER XIV.

ON THE ROAD.

Parting—Relief of mind—Night on Pea Ridge—Dead
bushwhackers—Preaching—Our appearance at the close of
our trip—Disappointment—Daylight.

SOON after the events narrated in the preceding chapter,
a supply train for the army came down from Springfield, Mo.
When it was ready to return, I made application to Col.
Harrison, commander of the post, who kindly placed one of the
wagons at my disposal, and afforded me all possible facilities for
our journey. In this was placed our trunks, bedding, and provisions; our few friends came around us, friends true and tried; my
wife and children took their places in the wagon, we parted from
our weeping friends, like them weeping, left home and the fruits
of a life's labor behind and started for we knew not whither. I
came to Fayetteville a few years before possessed of a handsome
competency. My investments for the support and comfort of my
family seemed judicious, but all was now to be abandoned, and
one hundred dollars was all I had with which to seek a home
and begin life anew. It was the 9th of February; my family had
been tenderly reared; how they would stand the exposure of a
journey North, where Winter still reigned, was a problem to be
solved; but my wife spoke bravely, the children were delighted
with the novelty; and our train with a strong escort of cavalry
set out for Missouri.

For some time before leaving my mind had been so agitated
by the scenes through which I had passed, and the gloomy

prospects of the future, that my health had suffered severely; my sleep was broken and unrefreshing, and I felt as if I should never relish food again; but scarcely had we lost sight of our old home before I experienced a sense of relief, and the first night out, with a wagon cover between me and the sky, I found rest in sleep, to which I had long been a stranger; my appetite returned, and before long I could eat the coarsest food with a keen relish, and nearly as much of it as the stout Irishman who drove our team. The country between Fayetteville and Springfield had been devastated by the armies which in rapid succession had passed to and fro; most of the houses had been burnt, their unsightly ruins meeting us nearly every mile, the fences destroyed, the cattle killed, and in the seven days and nights passed between the two points above mentioned, I did not hear a single chicken crow— a slight circumstance, but one which tells how utter and complete the destruction had been. As some of the ground over which we passed has become historic, I will briefly notice some of the scenes and incidents of a journey made under circumstances never to be forgotten.

The first night we halted at Holcomb's farm, once a beautiful place, but now deserted; Gen. Rains with his Missourians had encamped near there for some weeks, and his ragged and hungry command had stripped the place of every thing that could be used by man or horse; the owner was a secessionist, and it must have been most mortifying to have had his large and beautiful farm ravaged by Southern men. Some rails had been left, and these soon were blazing in perhaps one hundred camp-fires, for we had a large train and escort, quite a number of refugees, and a long ambulance train filled with soldiers, either slightly wounded or convalescent from serious illness; some of them on their way home, others to rejoin their regiments. The scene was somewhat exciting to be thus in the midst, and to form part of a camp; but after a long conversation at one of the fires with officers and other refugees, I sought shelter in the wagon where my family were sleeping, and found there a more untroubled sleep than I had known for a long time. With me the suspense was now over, for though I was on my way I knew not whither, yet I felt that the ties which had so long bound me to the South were severed at last, and the world all before me in which to seek a home.

The buoyancy of my own spirits astonished me. On thus leaving the fruits of years of toil, the energy of my early manhood in a measure departed; with little hope of ever retrieving my fortunes, a shade of sadness might have been expected; but no, a great weight had been taken from my heart; I was on my way to a land of free speech, to cast my lot with those whom I firmly believed to be in the right; my wife was happy at the thought that the scene of so much suffering and painful anxiety was behind us; my own heart remembered gratefully that Providence which in so many instances had shielded us, and in the full faith that the same kind hand would lead and protect us still, I could not be sad. The bugle sounded before dawn; I sprung from a deep and refreshing slumber, and soon at one of the camp-fires I was assisting in preparing the morning meal. This dispatched, our long train was soon in motion, and evening found us upon classic ground. To a train large as ours, good water, and plenty of it, was a necessity, and of this we had no lack, for our camp-fires that evening were lighted upon the banks of a beautiful and clear stream called Sugar Creek, upon the very spot where less than one year before a portion of the Southern army encamped the evening prior to the battle of Pea Ridge. Indeed, it was a part of the battle-ground itself; just above us on the opposite side of the stream, and full in sight, were the rude breastworks formed from the trunks of trees, from behind which the Federal batteries poured forth destructive volleys upon the enemy in the valley below; traces of the fierce strife were still visible, and Minie balls were still to be found in abundance.

Many of the wounded soldiers in our company had been present at the fight, and could point out places where the contest had raged; and in fighting over their battles they forgot how the night was departing, and a number of them, fine singers, struck up about midnight "Old John Brown;" I had never heard the song before, and its effect at midnight, sung by the voices of those who had on the same spot one year since joined the fierce battle-cry, was highly exciting; and when the chorus, "Glory, glory, halleluiah," pealed forth, it sounded like the most triumphant praise that I ever had heard. To hear a regiment starting from their homes to the battle-field, singing "as we go marching on," must have an effect most inspiring; but to hear the heroes on the very field upon which they had so proudly triumphed, at midnight, singing with proud emotion "as we go marching on," gave me a better idea than I ever had before of the song of conquerors.

The next day we traversed miles of the famous battle-field to which I have already alluded, and at some points saw striking evidences of the fierce struggle which had taken place. This was especially the case near the famous Elk Horn Tavern, which almost disputes with Pea Ridge the honor of giving the name to this hard-fought field; large limbs cut from the trees, and the massive trunks themselves shattered and riven by cannon-balls, as if by lightning, the underbrush mowed down by the destructive fire, suggested the sad fate of hundreds who for three days were exposed to that leaden and iron hail. Nor were the illustrious living and the glorious dead of that field forgotten; as our train wound slowly along the ridge dead comrades were brought to mind, and gallant officers praised by those who wore themselves the scars of that battle, and, in addition to them, the more recent wounds, yet unhealed, of Prairie Grove. One, I well remember, of the 37th Illinois, had been shot through the leg at the former battle, and now, with the other disabled at the latter field, managed, though on crutches, to get along as fast as the rest, and really seemed merrier than any one there. A Scotchman, with two or three wounds upon him, an intelligent fellow, spoke of his mother in the Old Country, who knew not of the dangers through which her son had passed; men of Kansas, Iowa, Wisconsin, Illinois, and nearly every nationality across the water were there.

We passed through Cassville the next day; it bore the usual evidences of military occupation; it had changed hands several times already, and every change was attended by destruction; the fences gone, dead animals strewn thickly around, and a general air of neglect and ruin pervaded the place. At night we camped at the Winter-quarters of Gen. Totten's Division, and felt a far greater sense of security than we had done on any previous night; for, though we had quite a respectable escort, it was known that large bodies of Confederate cavalry were scouring the country, and a train like ours was a great temptation to them. Now, however, we were surrounded by quite an army, and secure from all danger of attack or surprise.

Many of the convalescent soldiers with us here found their old companions in arms, and their greetings were warm and boisterous. It has been thought that camp-life hardens the heart and represses the finer emotions and sympathies of our nature; and while it must be conceded that facing death often, and familiarity with wounds and bloodshed, makes men look with comparative indifference on what once was appalling, yet no stronger friendships are formed than those which spring up between those who stand shoulder to shoulder in the deadly strife; and I have seen some of those veterans familiar with all the hardships and dangers of the war exhibit a tenderness and care for their sick and wounded comrades that was really womanly.

The next morning, passing through the camp of the 6th Missouri Cavalry, I saw a young soldier who had spent about a month under my roof, waiting upon a sick comrade who was brought to my house in almost a dying condition; and a sister or mother, it seems to me, could not have shown more tender and devoted care. The sick man recovered, and was then absent from camp on a foraging expedition, and his captain said he was the best man in his company. That night our camping-ground was on a large prairie, far from any timber; but there was a fine farm, well fenced, close at hand, and though it seemed a piece of vandalism to destroy property so valuable, yet there were sick and wounded men, and numbers of women and children, who must have suffered that bleak night; and, as men are not wont to reason long under such circumstances, the rails disappeared rapidly. This, however, is one of the inevitable results of war, and I suppose that none would expect men to freeze or starve when food and fuel were in sight and reach; and, indeed, when one comes to the trial, what, under other circumstances, would seem most wanton and unjustifiable, becomes almost a duty. The next morning we found the roads dreadful; six mules could scarcely pull empty wagons through the mud, in which the wheels sank to the hubs; a mile would sometimes require hours to accomplish it, but in the afternoon we found better roads.

On that day, soon after we had passed through a little village, some of our company, who were walking in the woods a short distance from the road, came running to the train, saying, that two men were lying dead in the brush not far distant; we went out to see, and there in the leaves lay two stout, desperate-looking men, dead; they had been killed an hour or two before, and were said to belong to a gang of bushwhackers who had infested that vicinity. Near the dead men lay their provisions, which they had procured from friends in the neighborhood; but it was a shocking sight to see human beings shot down, and left where they fell for beasts or vultures to prey upon. I had been among the dead time and again, till I was somewhat familiar with death, but never had death seemed so dreadful and repulsive as now. And yet they, doubtless, richly deserved their fate; had they not been slain some of the unarmed and defenseless ones in our train might have fallen by their hands; they were waylaying the road along which our train had to pass, and could, from the thicket in which they were concealed, have fired upon us with impunity. As we heard the story, they belonged to a band of six upon which a party of cavalry had come, killing these two, wounding a third, and taking two prisoners. The prisoners were brought into the village near—which was a military station— just as our train was passing through. One of the soldiers stopped at a house to get some provisions for his mess, some of whom were wounded men; he found no one in but a woman who said she had nothing for them, although he proffered liberal pay: he then asked her if she would cook some provisions which he had with him for his companions; this she likewise refused in a rude manner: he then asked her where her husband was; she replied, in the Southern army: how long since she had seen him; six months, she replied. At this moment the cavalry-men rode by, with the prisoners they had just taken walking before them. She uttered a loud cry; one of them was her husband, and she confessed he had been at home the night before to get some provisions.

This case is the history of hundreds; and the bare, black-ened chimney-stacks, which all along the road were the only wreck left of what once were happy homes, were the result of the fearful retribution which cases like that to which I have alluded had called forth. The soldiers had learned that, in most instances, the wretches who fired upon them from the *brush* were mostly fed at the houses near the place of their conceal-ment; and whenever a shot was fired at a courier or any one in the military service, the house nearest the place was burned, in some cases perhaps unjustly, but in many instances, though swift, it was a just judgment, perhaps the only remedy of which the case admitted.

The next day we reached Springfield, which but a short time before had been attacked by a large rebel force under Marmaduke; the convalescents, however, rallied from the hospitals to the aid of the few troops that were there, and repelled the assault. While there I met with one of the agents of the Sanitary Commission, who had seen and known me at Fayetteville, while he was there ministering to the wants of the brave men who had been wounded at Prairie Grove; he kindly proffered me any aid in his power, and urged upon my acceptance some articles calculated to render the remainder of our journey by wagon more comfortable. I accepted a part of that which was so freely and kindly offered, and I shall ever gratefully remember him and the noble association which he represented.

By Col. Carr, Chief Quarter-Master, I was kindly furnished with transportation for myself and family to Rolla; and from the beginning to the close of my journey I received the kindest attention, from officers of high grade down to wagon-masters and drivers, and should they ever see these pages, I trust they will serve to prove that their kindness is warmly remembered still. Men, too, whom I had never seen, offered me aid, which, though not accepted, was nevertheless grateful.

As we were traveling through a comparatively peaceful country we had no armed escort, yet at various points on the road we saw evidences of the strife which had raged not very long since through the region we traversed; and the traces which war leaves in a country through which it passes are unmistakable— the wanton destruction, the waste, the farms despoiled of fences, the villages shorn of their neat inclosures and shrubbery, traces of campfires at frequent intervals, dead mules and horses by the road-side, blackened ruins, and the general air of ruin and neglect, form a picture that once seen can never be forgotten. On the 20th of February we crossed the Gasconade, and camped for the night on its banks; the spot was very heavily timbered, and the campfires scattered over several acres, each surrounded by a company of characters the most varied, presented a spectacle of singular interest. After supper I was invited to preach, and seldom has preacher had a stranger audience than mine— the war-worn and disabled veteran; the soldier, faint and feeble with disease contracted in the camp; the merry-hearted but profane teamsters, and the sad-hearted refugee, with wife and children, seeking sorrowfully a home among strangers, together with a few persons living in the vicinity, formed a group worthy of the study of the painter, the moralist, and the Christian.

Knowing that it was of the first importance to fix the attention of my motley auditory, I began by bringing up home and the joys of early life, and I soon found that I had struck the right chord; few or none of them, I felt assured, had been destitute of early religious training, and they went back many of them in fancy that night to their pure and sinless days; they thought of pious parents, of godly examples, and strange was the contrast between their former and their present selves. I had a serious and deeply-attentive hearing; and that night, instead of the thoughtless profanity of the camp, the woods rang with old remembered words sung to old tunes, both of which my remarks had called up, the first time perhaps for years; the mules received their corn that night without the usual accompaniment of oaths which had become habitual, and the thoughtless, for the time at least, became thoughtful. I made no set sermon; I talked to them kindly and affectionately, as I most truly felt—appealed to the better nature which I felt was in every one of them; the thanks which were tendered me at the close I felt were sincere, and the recollections which I awakened in their minds made them, for that night at least, better men. Many audiences, rich, gay, and fashionable, that I have addressed, have faded or will fade from my memory, but never will pass away the recollection of that singular but attentive audience which I addressed that night beneath the open sky, with the glowing stars above, and the gleaming camp-fires all around, amid the lordly sycamores on the banks of the Gasconade.

At length, after fifteen days of wagon life, amid all the varieties of weather, from Spring-like to the most Wintery, with changes more like those which take place in dreams than in reality; amid a constant change of scenes and incidents, we reached Rolla, the railroad, and civilization. Were I able, I should like to reproduce the appearance we presented, but this a photograph could only fitly represent. The wagon had been our home for more than two weeks; our ablutions were performed at the nearest stream to our nightly encampment; changes of clothing were not to be expected in such a mode of life; my own garments bore very marked traces of the muddy roads we had passed, my wife's faded wrapper was torn by the bushes and briers through which we had often to walk when the roads were worse than usual; the garb of the children would have been a perfect disguise had I met them unexpectedly; a piece of blanket over the head and fastened under the chin was the head-dress of one of them, my own a cap of days long past, that of my wife and the other child I am at a loss to describe. From thence to St. Louis was but a few hours' ride, and there we expected to meet our old and tried friend Judge Tebbetts, who had been notified that we were on our way, but having been greatly delayed, he supposed we had taken some other course, and when we made our way to the Planters' House, to our sorrow we learned that he had started that morning to Springfield, and we had passed each other on the way. Seldom had I met with such a disappointment; but this would have been lessened very much had the clerk handed me a letter which I afterward learned was placed in his hands for me, directing me to join his family at their residence in St. Charles county, where our rooms were all prepared in expectation of our arrival, and hearts ready to welcome our coming; not only so, but the same letter authorized me to draw for any funds that I might need; in a word, it was just such a letter as only a true and tried friend could write; but failing to receive it, I knew not what course to pursue; a few days' stay in the city would exhaust our slender means; and though I met with an old friend whose greeting was as cordial as sunshine, I still was deeply despondent, and none the less so for being in a crowded city a stranger. I remembered that in former years I had friends in Cincinnati, and the thought that it would be the best point of outlook determined me to go there.

I acted upon the thought; and though my wife and children were entire strangers, I found that the friends of my early life were friends still, and friends to those strange ones I brought with me. Kinder greeting, more cordial welcome could not have been given, and we soon felt that after the long night of trial, danger, and anxiety, the dawn had come at last.